CW01655393

A History of the Metropolitan Railway

Rickmansworth to Aylesbury

including Halton Camp Railway

Lamplight Publications

260 Colwell Drive, Witney, Oxon OX28 5LW

First published 2004

© Lamplight Publications and Bill Simpson

All rights reserved
No part of this book may be reproduced, stored in a retrieval system or transmitted in any form or by means electronic, mechanical, photocopying, recording or otherwise without prior approval of the publishers

ISBN 1 899246 07 X

Designed and typeset by Lamplight Publications.
Printed and bound by the Alden Press at Oxford

A History of the

METROPOLITAN RAILWAY

Rickmansworth to Aylesbury

including Halton Camp Railway

by Bill Simpson

Lamplight Publications

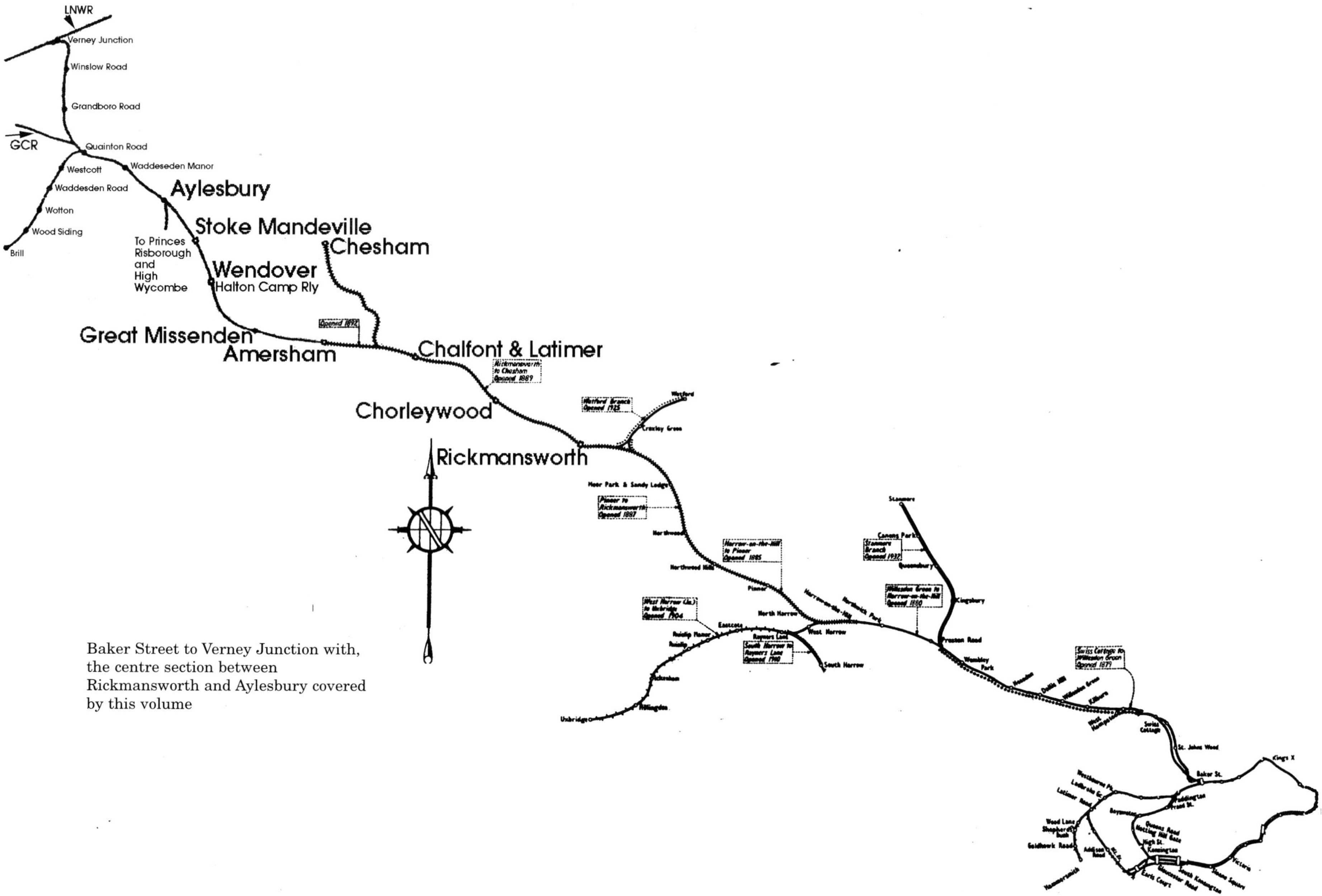

Baker Street to Verney Junction with, the centre section between Rickmansworth and Aylesbury covered by this volume

Foreword

This volume of my history of the Metropolitan concerns the hinterland between the city and remoter regions of north Buckinghamshire. It is as if the Metropolitan became another railway, comparing the crowded smoky confines of the sub-surface line in London, hurrying around a continuous circle, to spacious fields and tall wooded hills. Although operationally it is of course very much one railway.

Beyond Rickmansworth the line has to deal with continuous gradients rising into the Chilterns with a fleet of robust tank engines that carried the commuters and freight back and forth from towns that began as little more than villages. The Metropolitan was to change all of that, with substantial stations serving expanding communities. That being said, good design and thoughtful planning created an appealing mix of suburbia and country in a very unique way.

The arrival of the Manchester, Sheffield & Lincolnshire Railway, later Great Central Railway, in the late 1890's brought a new concept to the suburban Metropolitan. It was an alliance with some confusion, with the role of both railways being very different. Under the chairmanship of Sir Edward Watkin, of both railways, with his plans and grand designs to find the great way from the north, to the south coast. Neverthless they are also years of consolidation for the entire area, with the GCR forming an alternative alliance with the Great Western Railway, with both routes coming under the operational control of their respective Joint Committees which, largely speaking, produced the railways that still serve the area to this day.

Electricity was of course the great force of the twentieth century and an obvious one for the city. For the extension north the Metropolitan were able to take this only as far as Rickmansworth. It was to be the New Works Programme of the London Passenger Transport Board (1933), continued after the second world war, that saw power extended to Amersham.

One of the delights of the Metropolitan now is that its stations have not closed or lie little used, but are very much part of a busy commuter route and are particularly attractive north of Rickmansworth.

Bill Simpson
Bicester 2004

Acknowledgments

I would like to make special mention of the friendship and support of Mike Crosbie. I would also like to acknowledge the dedicated work of the late Ken Benest who did so much to collate and contribute valuable material on London's railways.

The following have generously contributed time and material without which I could not have produced this volume and I am very grateful for this.

The work of the late Tony Coldwell, Bob Darvill (Industrial Railway Society), Eric Fenton, Secretary, (London Underground Railway Society), Francis Hanford, (Curator, Royal Air Force Museum at Halton Camp), David Hibbert (London Underground Railway Society), John Mock, Simon Murphy, (London's Transport Museum), Peter Nicholls, Dave Potter, Albin John Reed, Dudley Rudd, Tim Stevens, Robin Waywell, (Industrial Railway Society), Ron White (Colour-Rail). The staff of the Archive Office and Buckinghamshire Centre for Local Studies at Aylesbury. All Photographers are acknowledged beneath their contributions.

Contents

The view north entering Rickmansworth, the bay on the right was used by steam locomotives removed on the trains going south. The electric locomotives tended to stand near to the goods shed, often seen there on photographs. That was of course when electrification terminated at this station.

Brunel University Collection

Chapter One

Through the Chilterns

The Metropolitan Railway had never set out to be a major trunk railway, like the London & Birmingham and the Great Western Railways, being flanked on each side by each of these two companies. Charles Pearson's dream had been to remove street congestion and provide a fast trouble free access to all pedestrians and commerce across London. In this respect it had magnificently succeeded and it had been followed in its wake with many other schemes that began to cross the capital. The horrendous costs and disruption of 'cut and cover' excavations dealt an expensive blow from which the company tottered to recover. This ensured that such large schemes would not be undertaken in the same way again. Further expansion would be on the edge of technological development, with the deep tube railways penetrating underground using a tunnelling shield. This began with the opening of the City & South London Railway in November 1890.

The extension north at Baker Street, beyond immediate suburbia, was largely seeded in the imagination of one man - Sir Edward Watkin; he took up Chairmanship of the Metropolitan on August 7, 1872. It seemed that he could find no peace unless it was finding new projects and challenges to wrestle with. He had come to railways at an early age, working as Secretary of the Trent Valley Railway in 1845 at the age of twenty-seven. Later he joined the LNWR and worked alongside the notorious Captain Mark Huish. He achieved the higher echelons in 1854 when he became General Manager of the Manchester, Sheffield & Lincolnshire Railway, a northern company from origins that grappled with alliances and took the heavy burden of the notorious Woodhead Tunnel through the Pennines earning it the sobriquet, 'Money Sunk & Lost Railway'.

Watkin had at some point in 1860 endeavoured to impress the board of this company with the proposal of an extension of lines by whatever means to London. At first he sought to reach an accommodation with the Midland Railway that had itself only reached the capital via Great Northern tracks up until 1868. However this 'accommodation' was badly mauled by the House of Commons Committee to such an extent that further endeavour would be fruitless. He continued his ascent of the MS&LR becoming Chairman in 1864.

Not to be deflected Watkin tried to form an amalgamation with the Great Northern Railway under Edmund Denison and had it been successful it would have rendered the

William Pollitt
General Manager of the Manchester, Sheffield & Lincolnshire Railway and Great Central Railway 1886-1902.

awesome prospect of the M&SLR building their own line to London unnecessary. Subsequent problems with the Met may well then have been with the GNR. However parliament regarded the amalgamations of the large conglomerates as not being in the public interest by doctrine dedicated to laissez faire policy and was against creating monopolies. A situation arguably for good or bad according to who was making money and was not. Certainly expansion and duplication would have benefitted by some rigorous control to prevent duplication of lines. Amalgamation when it did come was, perforce, necessary with the outbreak of the first world war in 1914, leading to the consolidated grouping amalgamation of 1923.

As far as the Metropolitan was concerned, from his position there as Chairman, Watkin continued to push matters from the other direction, north, beyond what would soon be the London suburbs. He felt certain, that by purchasing land alongside the line, the housing of the new utopia would follow. In this respect he was right and the Metropolitan did indeed benefit from this move. However, by the time it reached Rickmansworth on September 1, 1887 the railway had reached well out into the Chilterns on the edge of certain very hilly territory and the shareholders were looking for a return rather than further large capital expenditure. This area had been crossed in the west, somewhat tenuously by the Great Western Railway by supporting an offshoot called the Wycombe Railway with a line to Aylesbury opened in 1863. From the same station a local company called the Aylesbury & Buckingham Railway, connecting Aylesbury remotely with the London & North Western Railway's Oxford-Bletchley line near Claydon. The GWR agreed to run the A&BR with their locomotives and carriages.

In the east the LNWR ran somewhat indifferently by the town of Aylesbury, serving it only with a single line branch of seven miles from their main line from the London to Birmingham at Cheddington. A branch that had, like others set out with greater hopes to be much more with a line to Oxford before the GWR. Unfortunately capital was hesitant in1838 and it was not to be.

Before Watkin became chairman of the Met he became Chairman of the South Eastern Railway in 1868, therefore glancing at the railway map of the time his grand design becomes evident, to link with a prospective channel tunnel or at least, cross-channel transportation. In this ambition he would not only be brought into conflict with the arcane world of railway plotting, but also with the monarchical establishment that viewed republican France with no little suspicion.

Just as Watkin had tried to link the MS&LR with the Midland so he tried to join the Met with the LNWR passing through Chesham. This is a bit like putting his head in the lion's mouth. The LNWR had pronounced their disfavour of another London link in 1845 when Sir Harry Verney, MP of Claydon House, Buckinghamshire, promoted the Buckinghamshire Railway. He had been so keen to see this railway constructed in a cruciform shape with a line from Bletchley to Oxford (1851), with a junction mid-way to take a line to Banbury (1850). Together with a southern arm to Aylesbury and Harrow, there to join the LNWR. This is interesting, using a route that the London & Birmingham had at first considered and where the subsequent Metropolitan line would go. What brought about failure of the Bucks Act for the Claydon to Harrow section is fairly obvious, as it had three tunnels along the

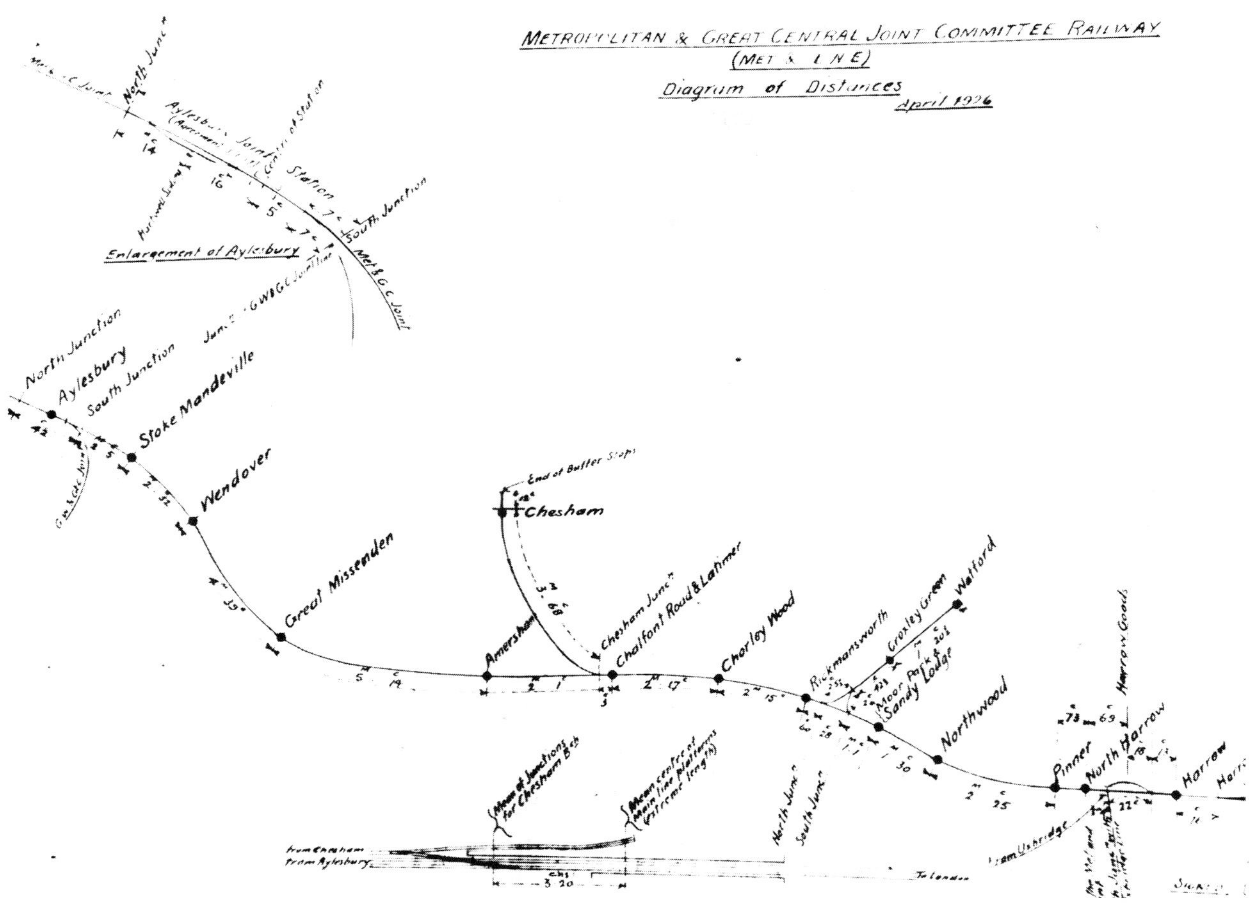

Distances on the line between Harrow and Aylesbury. The subsequent maintenance border line between the LNER, later British Railways and LT was on the 28½ milepost, just south of Great Missenden.

Mike Crosbie Collection

line, this tends to horrify investors. This proposed line left the L&B at Sudbury Station and passed on the west edge of Chalfont St Peter, then on the east of Chalfont St Giles. It then passed close by east of Amersham Church, thus avoiding the hill, continuing a little west of Great Missenden, then passing right through the centre of Wendover. Most remarkable at Aylesbury, crossing over at right angles the existing Aylesbury station, between the station and the locomotive shed. Presumably if the line had been successful the company would expect the LNWR to build a new integrated station on the site. Looking at tunnels of 570 yards near Uxbridge, 2057 yards between Amersham and Little Missenden and 1300 yards before Wendover, one can see straight away the pointless expense of it all that was obvious to the LNWR. As far as they were concerned the alignment of traffic north and south needed no more than their main line.

Before Watkin reached this part of the Chilterns further schemes were floated. Another independent concern called the Uxbridge & Rickmansworth Railway of June 28, 1861 promoted a line from the GWR near Cowley on the Uxbridge branch to join end on to the LNWR proposed Rickmansworth branch. This failed but recurred as the Rickmansworth, Amersham and Chesham Railway, including a branch to Chesham. This also faded away, until 1863 when it appears again, this time including a line to Aylesbury through Wendover. This faired no better than before.

In 1881 the LNWR promoted an Amersham & Chesham Railway extended from their Rickmansworth branch to Chesham. This was refused by parliament in favour of the Metropolitan Railway's Aylesbury, Rickmansworth Railway. The Chesham branch had been where Watkin had at first hoped to join with the LNWR near Tring, probably to avoid the earthworks north of Rickmansworth delineated in the Buckinghamshire Railway scheme. The eventual survey taken by the Rickmansworth & Aylesbury Railway carried the line high enough to place Amersham station on a hill, thus avoiding tunnelling. Watkin may well have been overplaying his hand with the LNWR, with the quarrelling in 1868 on the shared station in his native Manchester on behalf of MS&LR, this may have soured rela-

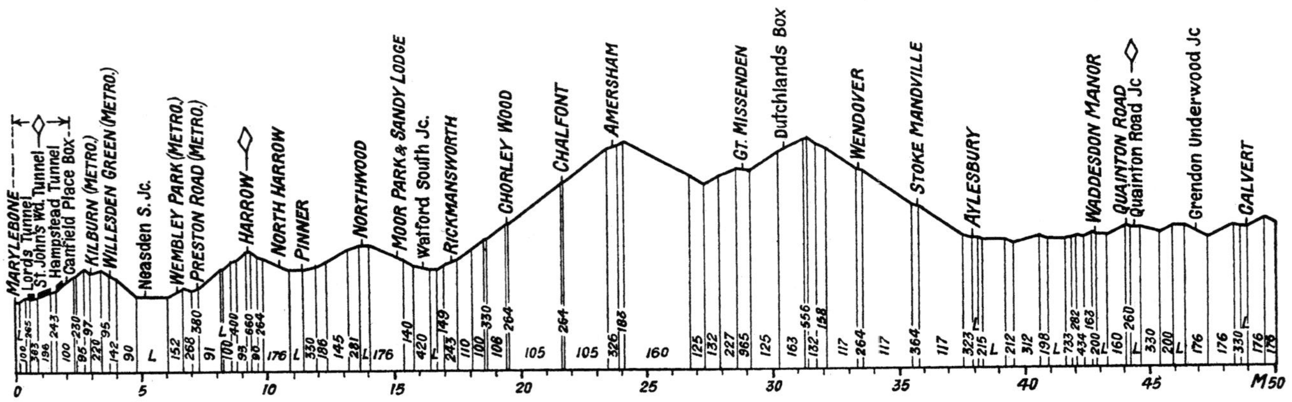

Gradient profile for the line from Marylebone to Calvert, note the severe climb beginning at Rickmansworth.
Railway Magazine

tions. Whatever, this plan came to nothing and Watkin was determined to seek some other outlet. He certainly would not let the opportunity for the town of Chesham slip out of his grasp, whether it be on a mainline or no, the station was being built to retain this option. It was sited half a mile short of its eventual site for which to advance it a separate Bill was needed. In all probability this was all that was left of the section Watkin had hoped would have been to Tring, letting the LNWR build the station.

His next attempt was on the advice of the Engineer Charles Liddell and the Duke of Buckingham, this was a curious option, to link up with an East & West Junction Railway, a rickety affair across south Warwickshire that had planned at the outset to tap the local iron ore traffic for South Wales. This came to nought and it now operated a line from Broom junction in the west, linking with the Redditch and Evesham line of the Midland Railway. On the eastern side connecting with the Northampton & Bedford line, also of the Midland Railway.

This line was joined by a Northampton & Banbury Junction Railway, that ran from Northampton to Banbury. What Liddel and the Duke proposed was that the Metropolitan should purchase the Aylesbury & Buckingham Railway connecting with the LNWR line near Claydon, thence be empowered to gain running rights over the branch to Banbury, where it would join the Northampton & Banbury line to Towcester, Northampton and Stratford-on-Avon at a place near Banbury called Cockley Brake Junction.

In this respect it made a great deal more sense than simply petering out at what became Verney Junction. Although the E&W and N&BJ had been engineered on a shoestring and would require extensive rebuilding. As things transpired it was a difficulty that did not reach the reckoning, as the Bill was thrown out of parliament twice. A second time as the Worcester & Broom Railway. This was probably with the LNWR's influence, across whose metals once again the Met would be obliged to find compromise by passing over the Banbury branch.

A possible link from Stratford to Birmingham made Stratford an interesting prospect which would bring it in conflict with the existing GWR connection. The notion now of the Metropolitan Railway providing a competitive railway to Birmingham seems bizarre. But like many unrealised schemes that flew about in all directions, it was not to happen.

Even so the Duke of Buckingham as Chairman of the LNWR and the Aylesbury & Buckingham Railway was still convinced and confided with Watkin on the prospect of a number of link lines using the A&BR as a launching pad. He probably saw, as it stands, the A&B a lost cause, unless it found further advancement, and it was a company that he had invested in. To be part of a London & Aylesbury Railway from Aylesbury to Rickmansworth, with an extension to Harrow, to which he wished to include a line to Princes Risborough from Wendover and instead of using the LNWR all the way to Cockley Brake Junction to build a new line from Buckingham to Towcester absorbing the E&WR network to move on to Birmingham from Stratford. This was in 1871. A syndication of lines was something that Watkin considered too attenuated, in reliance of the GWR and LNWR, relations with whom he already tried to foster. Neverthless trying to keep options alive Watkin addressed shareholders of the Metropolitan of a probable advancement to Birmingham and Nottingham. He was convinced that the Amersham Valley 'must be filled up'. That the need for railways had by no means been satiated and much was still needed. Not a point of view shared by established railways who saw duplication as deleterious to fruitful development.

At that time the A&BR was being run by the

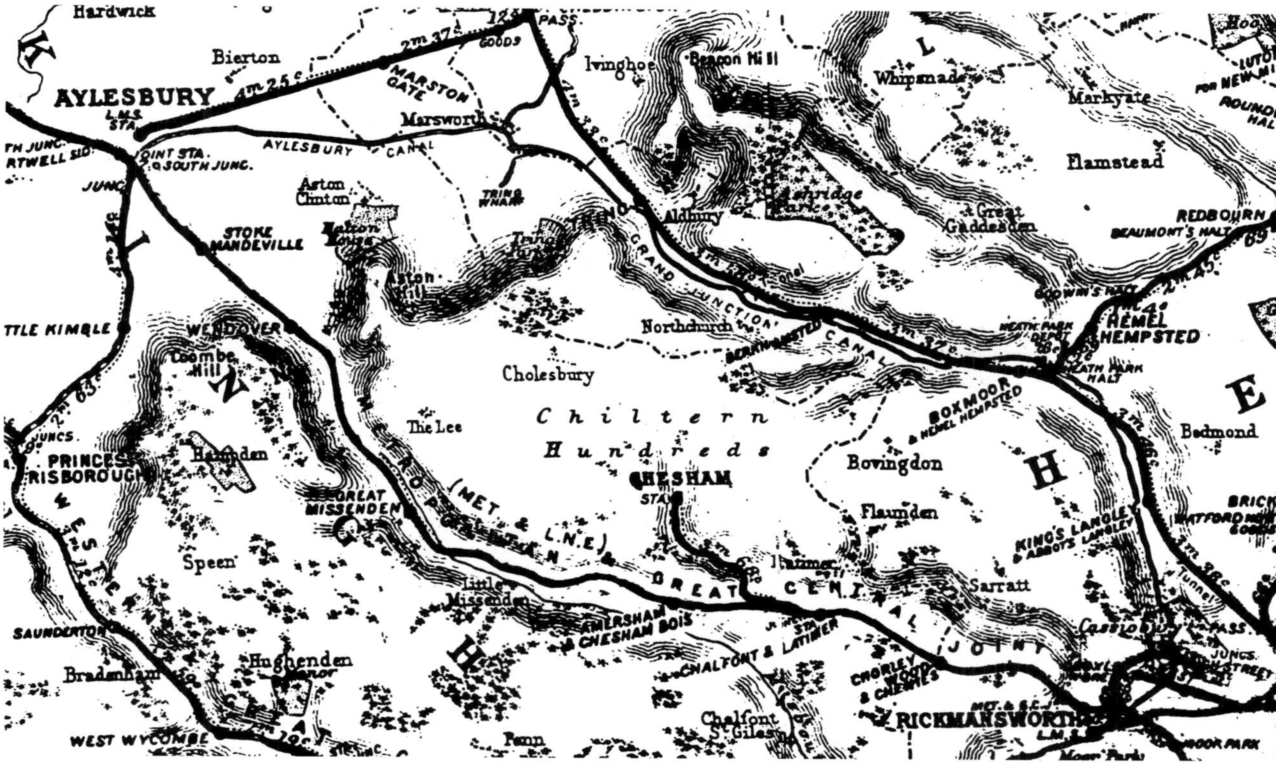

This LMS map gives a good indication of the 'wind' gaps in the Chilterns used by the railways. The older London & Birmingham Railway built their line via Hemel Hempsted and Berkhamsted, directly running by the rival Grand Junction Canal which caused a few fractious situations between them. The much later Metropolitan & Great Central Joint connected Rickmansworth, Chesham. and Aylesbury. Had Sir Edward Watkin succeeded in carrying the Met to end at Tring from Chesham it would have left the Great Central needing to build their London extension all the way down to Chalfont.

Bill Simpson Collection

GWR from the Wycombe Railway at Aylesbury in broad gauge. The A&BR having been constructed in the standard gauge. Fortunate for them the broad gauge at large was now in difficulties and the GWR were well aware that it could not survive so the line to Aylesbury from Maidenhead was a useful test ground for conversion. This the GWR did making them a greater competitor at Aylesbury, although they showed no signs of wanting to purchase the A&B.

The Worcester & Broom as part of the Duke of Buckingham's 'link lines' system did try this, but the A&B having got wind of Watkin's expansion held out lucratively for the arrival of his London company. The Duke then became preoccupied with other events as he took up the governorship of Madras. When he did return to live in the locality it was for a short time, as he died in 1889.

The A&BR was never a success, it was poorly managed and saw no more than three trains each way daily. Eventually it went into receivership. The Metropolitan purchased the line in 1891 from an Act of July 1891 with 3% guaranteed from 1894.

Driving on in his ambitions to build that new main line of railway north - south Watkin told the MS&LR that the Metropolitan could see the advantages of moving north to Aylesbury but a want of investment was creating inertia. What he wanted was the MS&LR and the SER to subscribe £50,000 to overcome this, both were in agreement in exchange for running powers. This apparent meeting of minds was tarnished by open rivalry between Pollitt of MS&LR and Bell of the Met. Seeing that his progress with the Met had been frustrated Watkin begins to realise that the MS&LR will have to build their own extension to London to meet the Met at Quainton Road on the former A&B. One cannot help but imagine that some of the directors of the MS&LR must have shuddered at the prospect. That they should build a London extension terminating in grand style in the capital, not forgetting that it could have considerable advantages in the future, if a tunnel was built under the Channel, with a continuous line to the continent. In this as in other schemes Watkin sought partnership with the Lancashire & Yorkshire Railway, another company without a London connection although their system in the north was almost as intense as the London one. Whatever, in the unrecorded discussions of Watkin this prospective arrangement disappeared.

Chesham has its rail communication at last, The public opening day of July 8, 1889 as the station is now open with a first train to Chalfont hauled by a small saddle tank, possibly a contractors engine loaned. The coaches are interesting, near the engine is one of the original coaches on the opening of the Metropolitan, with levelled off door tops. instead of the semi-circle type. The furthest coach with light coloured upper panels and window frames designates first class.

By 1883 he reported to the Metropolitan on the projected schemes north and in other meetings with the MS&LR spoke of the need for the extension south; between them all sorts of combinations were being expressed. In November 1884 there was a Banbury, Northampton & Metropolitan Junction railway for the link between Verney Junction and the East & West Railway, then there was the aforementioned Worcester & Broom with which Watkin had tried to access with the most economic prospect.

The first Bill for the London extension met a surprisingly concerted opposition from artists like Alma Tadema and uproariously the prospect of invading the hallowed sanctum of Lords Cricket ground. Predictably the Great Northern and the Midland put up their various cases for opposition, another line having a prospectively deleterious effect on their London services, which was subsequently to prove the case. The opposition must have brought sufficient weight to bear for the Bill was thrown out at the committee stage, with uncertainty of exactly why. Possibly the turmoil of the building of the Metropolitan, even though this tried to follow roads, remained as a harrowing memory. Unable to use street alignment, the new extension would have to cut across the existing suburban ring. It was now a long time since the 1830's when the original trunk lines had been built and London had much expanded beyond by then.

The Bill returned in 1892 presented by Watkin with modifications and much mediation behind the scenes. This time it successfully passed the Committee stage but fell into conflict with the London County Council in the Lords who wanted cheap trains for ten miles out of London and £750,000 for new streets and 11,000 population it would displace. Unfortunately the MS&LR was suffering the consequences of the roughshod way the earlier railways had cut through dense industrial housing as existed north of London. This delayed the Bill until the fall of the incumbent Conservative government bringing a General Election. Watkin complained to Lord Salisbury the Prime Minster, but to no avail, the Bill had to be held over for the next parliament and government.

After the election Watkin's powers of persuasion must have carried the day and the extension Bill received the Royal Assent in March 1893. It was to prove, for the MS&LR a pyrrhic victory.

Much has been written and published on the workings of this massive undertaking vividly chronicled with the capabilities of photography at the turn of the century. What became very clear was difference from the works of sixty years previously, with great lumbering steam machine excavators that looked more cumbersome than their worth, neverthless they made a huge difference. Earthworks with long embankments and wide sweeping cuttings pro-

One of the contractors engines working on the MS&LR works in London under the contract of Bott & Stenett an 0-6-0 saddle-tank called 'Gordon' at Neasden steam shed.

R M Casserley Collection

nounced this project as being so different to what had gone before. Contractors had their own temporary railway system to draw the spoil with tough little tank engines doing the work. The new line seemed to bestride the countryside of Leicestershire, Oxfordshire, Northamptonshire and Buckinghamshire like the first long distance motorway, the M1 was to do, just over fifty years later with elevations designed for continuous speed. This railway meant business in a big way, the problem was when speed arrived at the lesser engineered Metropolitan Railway with its gradients and sharp curves its whirling fortissimo became a ritual folk dance. The M&SLR made its connection with the Met at Quainton Road and became the Great Central Railway in 1897. Echoing earlier proposals it did connect up with the E&WJR near Byfield.

Uncertainty of the London extension is evident when sufficient capital funds had not been generated until 1894, a disastrous coal strike in the north seriously affected the MS&LR. It is as if the forces of providence warned the company that this was all folly.

Watkin's failing health had forced him to retire from all his chairmanships in January 1894, leaving the MS&LR to get on with the job of joining the Met at Quainton Road and bringing to a financial return the enterprise that he had initiated leaving a weighty baton to run with. He resigned his Hythe constituency in the 1895 General Election. He had created a main line connection north for the Met and south for the GCR of uncertain worth. A man of monumental influence, some would say pragmatic, had left the centre stage of railway development.

Two years after it's opening at Marylebone on April 13, 1899, in 1901, Watkin died.

The new Chairman of the Metropolitan in 1894 was a John Bell, somewhat against anticipation, as the progenitor who had worked with Watkin as a long serving director and confidant on both boards since 1872 was H D Pochin. Probably the effects of keeping pace with Watkin took its toll, as he died in 1895.

Bell did not appear so aggrandised to the grand situation of the mighty trunk line as his former boss, he would now have to live with the relationship of the Great Central Railway. It was to prove a thorny period for them both. What Bell did inherit was his boss' truculence and determination to have his way.

During its existence the Aylesbury & Buckingham Railway, had sprouted a six mile branch from Quainton Road to reach close to the village of Brill, largely on the demesne of the Marquess of Chandos, later Duke of Buckingham the man of the Aylesbury & Buckingham Rly, this also was now a part of the Met. It was a twig that held the germ of greater ambition, to extend to Oxford, with Metropolitan support. A Baker Street - Oxford railway is something to ruminate on as a might have been. But the pathway for this was blocked

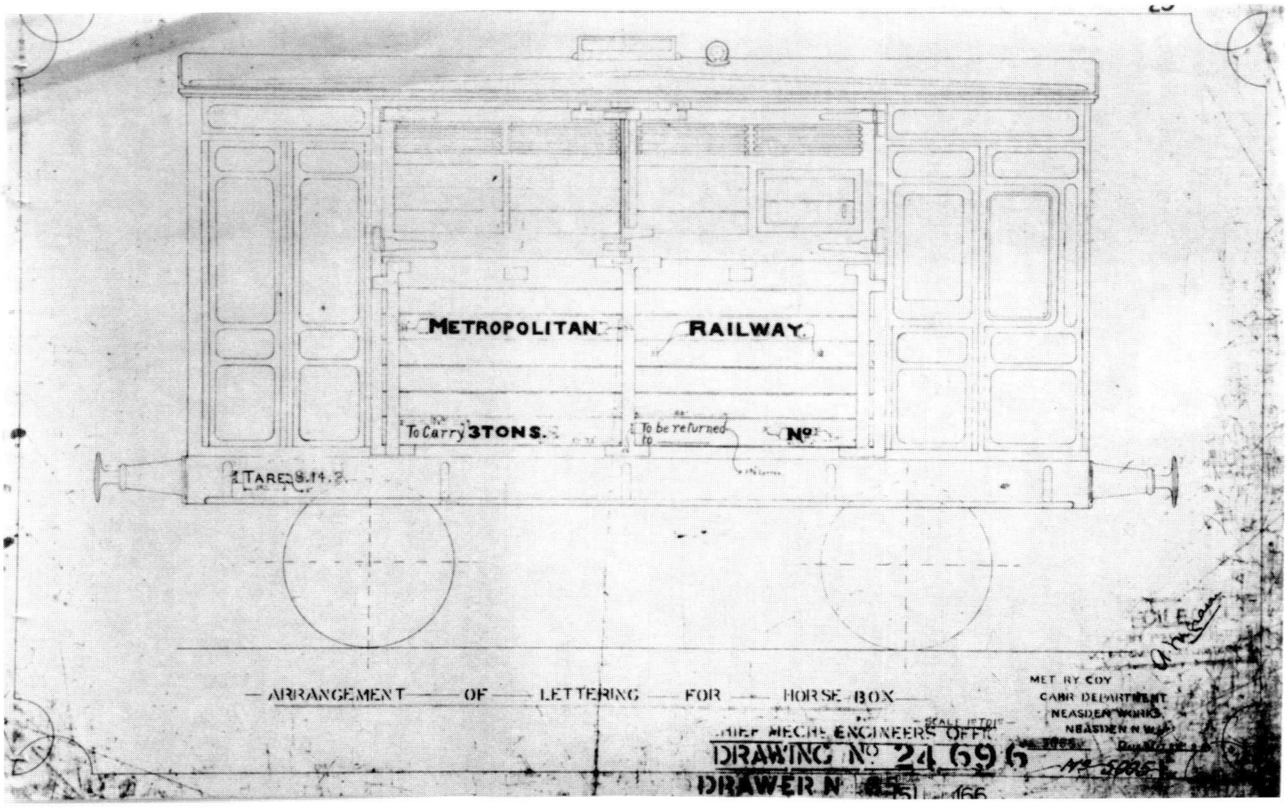

Drawing for Metropolitan horsebox, ten of which operated on the railway in the Chilterns. The drawing is dated for September 20, 1904

Mike Crosbie Collection

by Muswell Hill which overshadowed such a plan, needing a 1,650 yd tunnel. Had Watkin the time to employ his redoubtable energies to trying to drive this line through it would have proved historically intriguing. For instance would it have closed in 1935, and later electrification have stopped at Amersham?

As the Metropolitan progressed to Chorleywood and Chalfont Road (later Chalfont and Latimer), this being reached on July 8, 1889, it retained the line to Chesham as a branch but diverted its interests to the A&BR at Aylesbury. Chesham had drawn the not too unique conclusion, by that time, that any town that hoped to develop its economy would need good railway connection and Chesham was adept in manufacture. Therefore the Met was a gift to Chesham, even though it would have to be at the end of a three mile single track branch line. As an enticement, the town having made a gift of £2,000 to ensure purchase of a central site for the station. This was to avoid the proposed site some distance away. To this effect a Bill was lodged to extend the line closer to the town by a further half a mile. So Watkin got somebody to pay for something!

The working agreement with the GCR meant together with the Metropolitan a Joint Committee was formed in which the Metropolitan undertook to lease their line from Harrow to the north to Verney Junction, including the Chesham branch for £44,000 per annum for 999 years. They also agreed to lease the lines from Harrow South Junction to Canfield Place for £20,000 per annum. The Met were fairly canny in this arrangement that netted them an income from their lines, essentially when they themselves were not using them. That is to say they would protect that right with a clause to safeguard their lucrative suburban traffic. The Met stipulated that the lessees should have their first station outside London, to the west of the River Brent. Harrow on the Hill was chosen by the GCR 9¼ miles from Marylebone and Wembley Hill.

Not for the first time, in these situations, uneasy relationships evolve between heads of different companies. Bell had been an aide to Watkin as he worked as General Manager under his Chairmanship, but he was purely a Metropolitan man and he was determined to guard its interests. He probably did not feel that all his former boss' schemes had been necessarily in its best interests.

William Pollitt, General Manager of the GCR had, perforce to retain the best for GCR interests and these were not always going to be in perfect alignment.

An Act of 1895 made by the MSLR, with

little discussion with the Met, was to make a double track parallel to the Met between Wembley Park and Canfield Place, near Finchley Road station intended in place of a modest widening proposal in an Act of 1893 by MSLR for widening on north side of Met between West Hampstead and Finchley Road. This was designed to facilitate a connection with the LNWR and the docks. Bell resisted this whilst Pollitt maintained it was essential for MSLR as the traffic for Wembley Park could not be accommodated on the existing Met double track west of Finchley Road. Bell felt that any quadrupling to be undertaken should be done so by the Met and as a consequence advised his fellow directors to oppose this Bill.

The MSLR gave way and agreed to the Met doing the quadrupling provided the MSLR had exclusive use of the extra tracks and relinquishing its use of the Met tracks from the agreement of 1890. The Met agreed, providing that they retained control of access to Wembley Park goods yard and any other lands not purchased by the MSLR. This final agreement was sanctioned by an Act of July 6, 1895.

As it was necessary to rebuild overbridges to accommodate MSLR locomotives the Met decided to continue the work on to Harrow a further 2¼ miles. The MSLR understanding this applied for running powers on to Harrow to which the Met agreed but not for exclusive use.

The MSLR began construction of their own line from Canfield Place to Marylebone with spoil carried over the Metropolitan in eighteen trains a day to Neasden.

New structures to accommodate MSLR, were new intermediate signalboxes at Mantles Wood, on a gantry between Amersham and Great Missenden. Also at Dutchlands, between Great Missenden and Wendover and the expansion of Harrow Yard, all opened in 1900. In effect the arrival of the MSLR had forced the Met to put in hand alterations that would be desirable in any case, particularly extending the loading gauge dimensions which would enable stock from other companies, hitherto restricted from Met lines, to be accommodated. Also much of the freight requirements were installed to enlarge the capacity for this traffic at West Hampstead, Willesden Green, Harrow, Northwood, Chesham, Wendover, Stoke Mandeville and Quainton Road, all authorised from October 1897.

The first coal train ran over the junction at Quainton from MSLR July 26, 1898.

An example of the abrasive situation between Pollitt and Bell took place at Quainton as the GCR claimed its right to run coal trains off the Metropolitan at Aylesbury and on to the GWR to access London by that route. Bell regarded this as not following the 1890 agreement. The GCR decided to put it to the test in the early hours of Saturday July 30, 1898. Bell placed himself in the Quainton Junction box and saw to it that the signalman refused the train. Even though two days before the GCR had issued a writ preventing the Metropolitan from hindering such trains. The Met held the GCR to the agreement that the line was not fully open and on temporary licence therefore it must conform to the agreed route. As a result no coal trains were permitted on the GWR via Aylesbury until March 20, 1899. It was not until March 31, 1901 that all four lines were available between Harrow and Finchley Road and the GCR could take up exclusive use of its two roads on the south side.

The MSLR had at one point proposed to amalgamate with the Met but the parlous condition of its finances made this a most unattractive proposition to the London company.

In 1897 the MSLR and the GWR had reached an understanding for the line from Culworth Junction to Banbury after the GWR got the former to drop some hostile moves.

As the GCR, they realised that they would always play second fiddle in the Met partnership and decided, even at further cost, to find accord with the GWR. The latter company always regarded their Oxford route to Birmingham as too circuitous and sought a line from the Wycombe Railway's Princes Risborough station to Aynho Junction. Therefore in mutual need the GWR/GCR Joint Committee was established which would give the GCR access via a new junction at Grendon Underwood to Ashendon to access the GWR, then leave at Northolt to Neasden, completely independent of the Met.

This also gave them a much better engineered route into London. The Met were furious as this was not in the spirit of their agreement and tried to oppose it. However parliament was not dissuaded from granting these new powers and the Neasden - Northolt line was granted in the Act on August 12, 1898, with the Grendon Underwood line confirmed on the following year. The Met did exact some compensation for its expenditure from Finchley Road to Quainton Road to the extent that this would not be required for itself, should the MSLR decided to move most of their traffic over to the new arrangement.

The arrangement also heralded a new dawn in management of the Met and GCR Joint with a new General Manager of the Met, Abraham Charles Ellis and Sir Sam Fay of the GCR bringing the quarrellous period to an end. Although it must be no little credit to the GWR, with whom the alliance of 1906 had to some extent turned the tables on the Met, putting the GCR in a strong position. Whatever, the two aforementioned gentlemen were of much more agreeable and positive demeanour, realising that working together was for the benefit of all. Following a final settlement being drawn up and signed in 1907. This involved the GCR paying the Met compensation for under usage of its investment of works to accommodate the GCR. Consequently the GCR decided to introduce a suburban service of its own from Marylebone to Aylesbury and High Wycombe. This involved the use of comfortable modern stock of the GCR which compared with disfavour to the Met's earlier vintage. This fired the Met into producing their new 'Dreadnought' coach design.

Some disagreement came over the GCR using the Met's tracks at high speed especially with speed checks at Rickmansworth, Aylesbury and Quainton Road. The tragic outcome of this was the accident at Aylesbury where a 'down' newspaper parcels express passed over the 9-chain radius curve between the Met and the GWR south of the station and became derailed resulting in the death of the driver and fireman, plus another fireman travelling as a passenger. This was on December 23 1904. The circumstances of excessive speed would best be countered by altering the layout of lines and in any case the station had sustained considerable damage. Consequently the main line through the station was moved a few yards to the east, easing the curve and moving it a little closer to London. The station was under the joint ownership of the GWR, Met and GCR which only received its rebuilding in 1925-6 when the layout was again effectively altered up until former GCR line closure in 1966.

Diminishing returns on the Circle and local suburban lines of the Met due to the intensive competition of motor buses convinced the Board, lead by Robert Hope Selbie who succeeded Charles Ellis as General Manager in 1908, to encourage further growth of Metro-land. Ostensibly to bring lucrative first class ticket passengers out to live in the green acres beyond the city in houses built as part of developments of the Metropolitan Estates Commitee beyond Rickmansworth.

To this effect a new Pullman service was decided upon as part of an arrangement with the Pullman Car Company who would provide two new first class cars under the usual arrangements. The Pullman Car Company first introduced their cars in the country, as the first bogie stock to run on our railways, on the Midland Railway in 1874. In view of the history of the Met it is interesting to see the South Eastern & Chatham introduced cars on their system followed by the Metropolitan in June 1910. The cars were built by the Birmingham Railway & Carriage Co. They began running from the City to Aylesbury and Chesham, at the outset to Verney Junction. One was included in a midnight theatre train from Baker Street to Aylesbury. Known by their evocative names of 'Mayflower' and 'Galatea'. They were suspended during the First World War and on their return afterwards did not run to Verney Junction. They were finally withdrawn in 1939. Seen for a time in sidings at Hampton Court where they were removed from their bogies. The bogies were then sawn in half and carried off on flat wagons. The cars then went to became a wood merchants store/office at Hinchley Wood, Surrey. Finally being scrapped in 1948.

By all these works the rolling hills and beechwoods north of Rickmansworth were influenced, but not drastically changed. It was left to road transport to do that. Fine stations remain north of Rickmansworth that have melded into the countryside, which at Wendover and Great Missenden have been rawly dissected by a modern high speed by-pass. No doubt desirable for the towns involved, but another example of the automobile's 'increase of appetite that grows by what it feeds upon'. Neverthless, the railway competes efficiently and attractively.

The ticket office at Rickmansworth in 1934

London's Transport Museum

Chapter Two

Rickmansworth

Close to Rickmansworth the rivers Chess, Gade and Colne join and feed the Grand Junction Canal which passes south of the town. From this point north the landscape is characterised by wooded hills and clefts where the river courses from the Chiltern water shed drain through the 'wind gaps' south.

Various railway schemes, as explained in the opening chapter, fought and foundered on these slopes. The problem is clearly defined when from Rickmansworth to Amersham the line climbs continuously on a seven mile slog up a gradient largely of 1 in 105.

North of the town a tract of land was laid out for development by the Metropolitan Railway Country Estates Company. This land is called the Cedars Estate extending from the station on to Chorley Wood.

The station was opened on September 1, 1887 and the area around it was much enlarged in 1902 to take a lot of sand and gravel traffic, doubtless for the building expansion taking place alongside the line. Even this operated with some limitation and forced some goods to be handled at Willesden Green. There were considerable goods facilities at Neasden, Harrow and Willesden Green, that was until finally Eastern Region dispensed with all goods working which was removed to Willesden Junction in 1966.

Electrification of the Metropolitan from 1901 advanced through north London to reach Rickmansworth in January 1925 when the service began. From that point on electrification on this route had to wait until September 9, 1961. Requirements of funding and the end of World War Two being drastic setbacks until it could at last be carried to Amersham and Chesham. This meant that steam locomotives, now banished to lines north of Rickmansworth for passenger

One of the H class 4-4-4 tanks no 107 in 1934, possibly about to detach from its southbound train at Rickmansworth. Still lettered 'Metropolitan' although the Met has ceased to exist and all eight of the engines were sold to the LNER in 1937, renumbered 6415 - 6422 inclusive. London Transport abandoned the practice of painting 'Metropolitan' and replaced this with 'Met' in 1934. This identified them as such until it was replaced by 'London Transport'. The 4-4-4 wheel arrangement was not common in this country, only four pre-grouping railways built locomotives with it. The Wirral Railway who were first in 1896; followed by the Midland & South Western Junction Railway and the North Eastern Railway. A drawing for a Midland tank engine never materialised.

London's Transport Museum

work, had to learn a unique dexterity in transferring motive power at the station for 'up' and 'down' trains, particularly in the rush hour periods. This was done in no more than five minutes, often less, without any passengers being aware that it had happened. This animated scene continued on until the line was electrified to Amersham. This ended the period of steam for passenger working at the station. Previously this manoeuvre had of course been carried out at Harrow.

Appropriate signalling followed the process of electrification with the replacment of the 'lock and block' system, introducing electric automatic signalling with three colour light aspect and illuminated traffic indicator diagrams in the signal boxes. These show the whole of the track controlled by the box where the progress of the train is shown by a darkening movement of light to show the position of the train. This allowed the trains to speed up and follow each other more closely with automatic stops on any train that should pass a red signal due to the incapacity of the driver. Similarly, should a signalman be taken ill, the line will automatically fail safe to all signals at danger.

Although outside the period of the Metropolitan it is interesting to observe the continuity of the system which came with the London Transport's electrification scheme costing £9,000,000. This was for the electrification of lines from Rickmansworth to Amersham, including the Chesham branch. With the four tracking of the line from Harrow to Watford South Junction completed 1959-1962.

The extent of all this can be best appreciated with the rebuilding and widening of 13 bridges to take additional tracks and allow the width of roads above and below the railway to be widened.

An excellent study of no 53 'A' class locomotive in orginal form without cab. As the loco was scrapped in 1907 this would be before then. Note the original position of the numbers on the chimneys for identification passing through the tunnels. Also the Neasden destination board on the front.

R K Blencowe

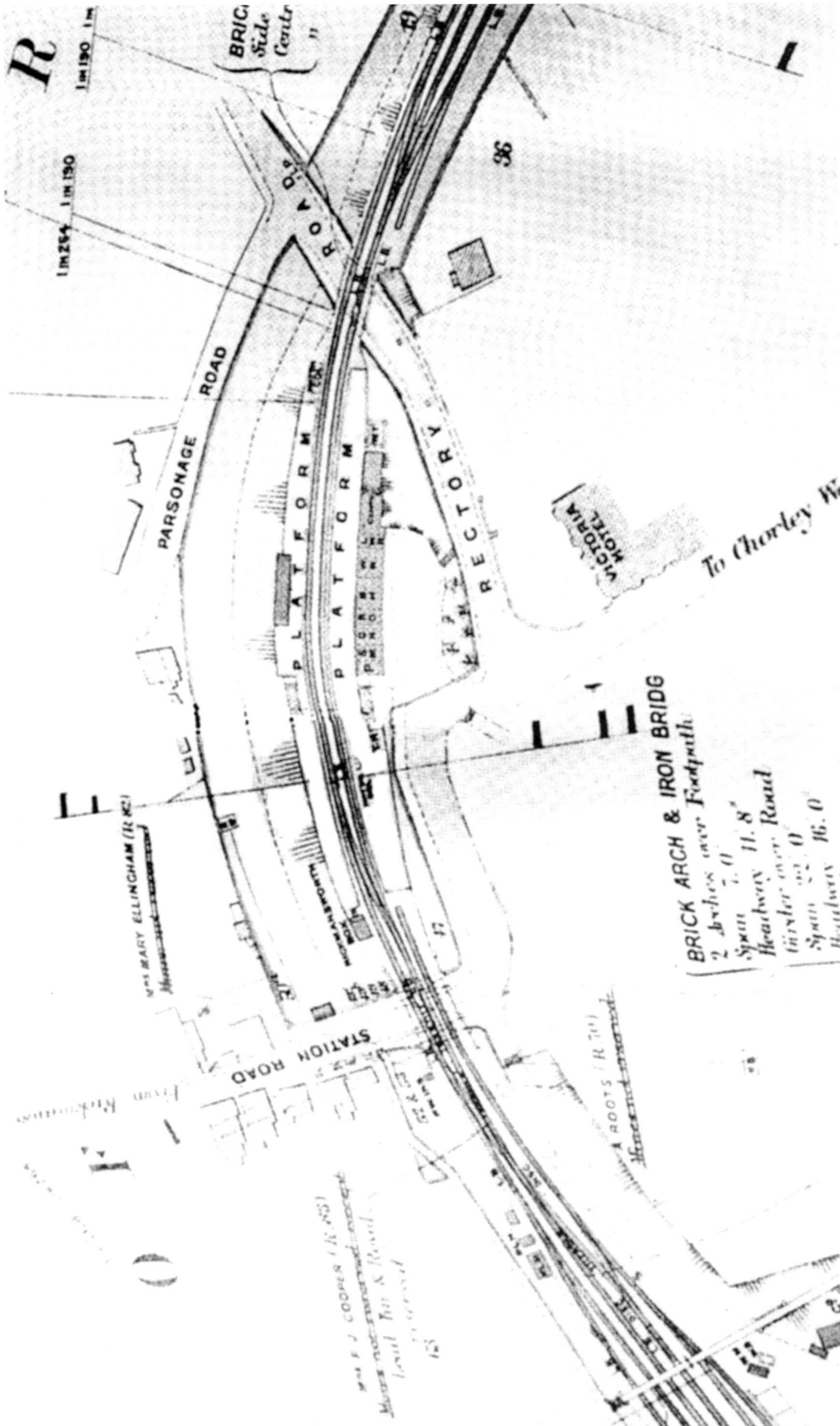

This Metropolitan & Great Central Joint Committee ground plan diagram gives a good indication of the severe curve at Rickmansworth which was such a contention for GCR trains having to slow down to a very low speed which would apply largly to Great Central trains as Met trains stopped.

John Mock Collection

Changeover completed south of Rickmansworth station with MetroVick loco no 16 'Oliver Goldsmith' having taken charge of a train for Liverpool Street from no 42134 Fairburn tank in 1961.
London's Transport Museum

Stationmasters together, in the centre is Jack Roberts who was a Met man for all of his life. He began his working life at Fenemore's Foundry at Brill but left there to work on the Brill Tramway. He later became Stationmaster at Rickmansworth and Wendover, living in retirement in that town where he died.

London's Transport Museum

MetroVick locomotive no 18 'Michael Faraday' having just relinquished the charge of its train to Aylesbury to a steam locomotive on July 22, 1955

H C Casserley.

T stock 2715 at Chorleywood in September 1961 running in place of A60 stock hence carrying no 99.
D M Hibbert

Chapter Three

Chorleywood

The station was opened here July 8, 1889. The name Chorley Wood was retained until 1915 when it was changed to Chorley Wood and Chenies until 1934. From that time until 1965 it reverted back to Chorley Wood and then changed to its present title of Chorleywood. It is a place of outstanding natural attraction that so closely identifies with the image of city gent turned countryman in the new commuter age. A leading proponent of this was the artist architect Charles Voysey who designed in detail the villa style for these beech woods. The Metropolitan Railway Country Estates Ltd built detatched residences on plots of land one acre and more comprising of more than six hundred acres between Rickmansworth and Chorley Wood. This came to be known as the Cedars Estate. Assured spacious havens of domestic harmony, with London but thirty-two minutes away by rail.

The stations themselves from Rickmansworth north take on a distinctive and very attractive design. The long extension of deep valances are replaced with ridged gables facing the tracks. Steel trusses and beams support them with cast iron columns with decorated capitals and fluted shafts. Largely speaking the same building pattern is maintained throughout with single story station buildings of robust brick and tiled roofs with finials on each gable peak.

Immediately facing the front of the building is the Chorley Wood Hotel, see ground plan. This is a fine building which suggests an important role from earlier days, now long past. It is in the country villa style so familar in the Chilterns and stands importantly to the unassuming single storey building of the station.

Chorleywood signalbox 1979, unused but as yet not dismally boarded up.
Brunel University Transport Collection

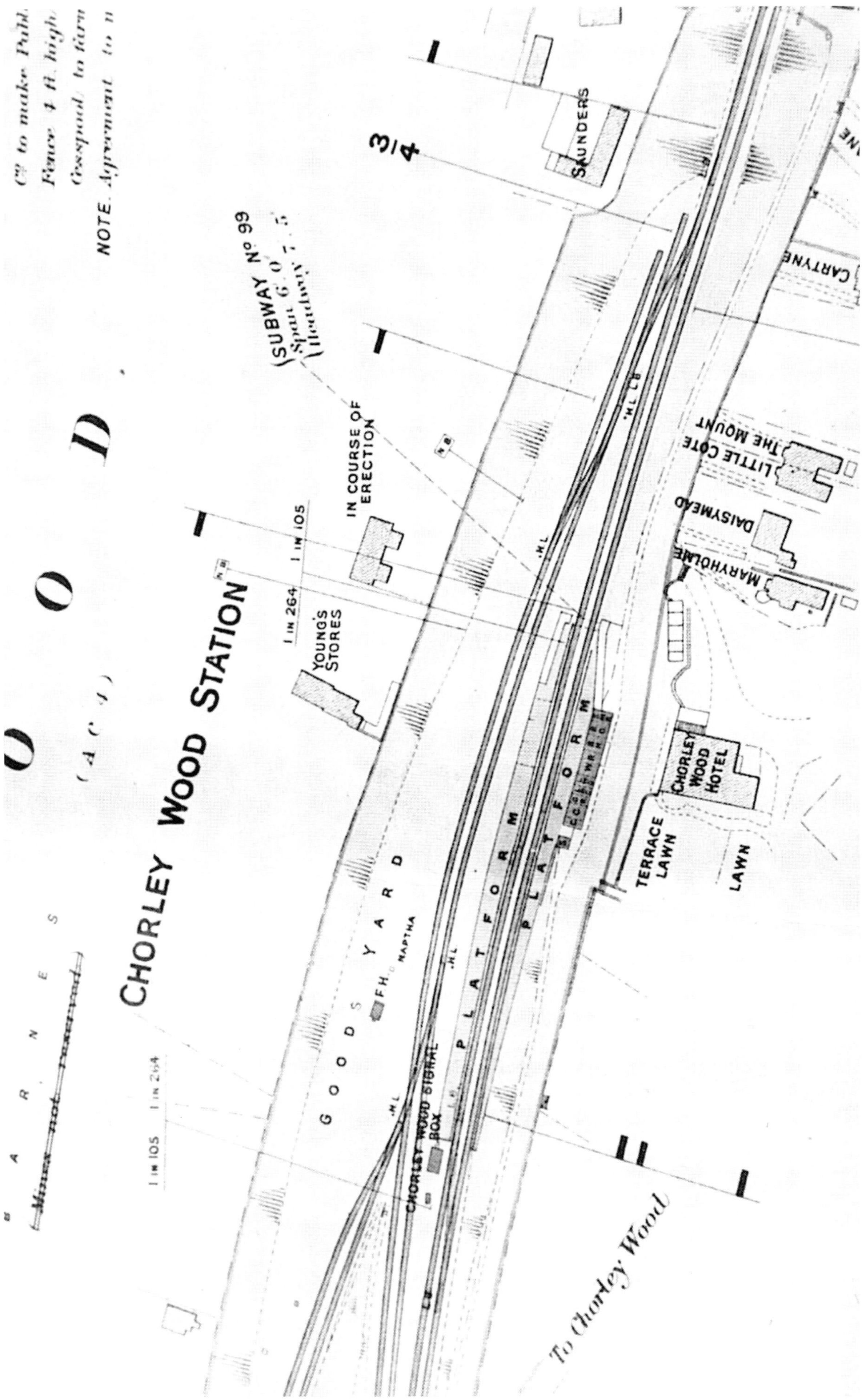

Chorleywood station facing the imposing Chorleywood Hotel in 1908. Note the subway connection between platforms.

John Mock Collection

Under gaslight, the station ticket hall and entrance at Chorleywood in 1944. On the far platform amongst the films advertised is one of Eric Portman in 'A Canterbury Tale'.

London's Transport Museum

A visit at Chorleywood with a T stock hauling the gauging train that came out from Acton and as required would cruise around the system, testing platform clearances especially.

London Underground Society

An 'H' class 4-4-4T no 110 near Chorleywood hauling the superbly lined out Metropolitan train, the coach number is 443.

H C Casserley

This view of the goods yard at Chorleywood on August 25, 1960 shows how the facilities had developed prior to electrification north to Amersham. They were now for the use of British Railways only.

Albin J Reed

Chorleywood looking north August 29, 1959. Note the footbridge on the left to cater for railway staff to walk over British Railways lines.

R M Casserley

Chorleywood front, plain, but smartly business like. The buildings north of Rickmansworth have little ornamentation, this is left to the canopies. The station buildings were little more than housing architecture being initiated by the Metropolitan Railway Country Estates Company in the townships developing alongside the route.

Bill Simpson

One of the unenviable jobs from the days of steam, cleaning out the soot from the smokebox of the engine at Neasden on March 11, 1933. This E Class 0-4-4 engine survived up until 1963 when it was withdrawn and scrapped in the following year.

H C Casserley

From below street level in London, to similar confines in Liverpool, as Met 4-4-0 tank 'Orion', one of the original eighteen that worked the Met Circle at the beginning then lived out its final days on the Mersey Railway. Although this railway was electric this engine hauled around engineering supplies on the system, unscheduled, a wanderer that had known hectic days.

Liverpool Daily Post

A southbound train entering Chalfont station behind 'H" class 4-4-4T 109 with a train of 'Dreadnought' stock in the 1930's.
R K Blencowe

Chapter Four

Chalfont and Latimer

Along with Chorley Wood this station also was opened on July 8, 1889 and known first of all as Chalfont Road until 1915 when it was changed to Chalfont and Latimer. It has the role of being the junction station for the branch to Chesham which runs parallel for just under a mile before winding its route along the valley of the Chess.

Chalfont has now practically overlapped in development with the larger town of Amersham and if one sits on the left side of an Aylesbury train it is a visual delight to ride on the heights of the beautiful Misbourne Valley.

Much of the development along the line had taken place at Willesden Green, Harrow and Wembley before and after the first world war. The rolling affect of this was that north of Rickmansworth started to develop in the later 1920's and 1930's. Chalfont had a substantial post office building opened in 1935 not far from the station. It was at this time that the extension of electrification became a neccessary pre-requisite to these new settlements. However, the huge demands made upon the new London Passenger Transport Board, established by the Act of 1933 for improvements on the London Transport system and the dislocation of the second world war meant that this did not become a reality until 1960. In consequence the steam hauled services north of Rickmansworth had to cope for nearly thirty years longer than the Board would have preferred.

The transition, a 'Dreadnought' stock 1st to London Transport. These handsome coaches were introduced by the Metropolitan before the first world war to counter the superior stock used by the GCR on their new suburban service. No doubt the name came from the topicality of the time, that being Lord Fisher's design of super battleship.
H C Casserley

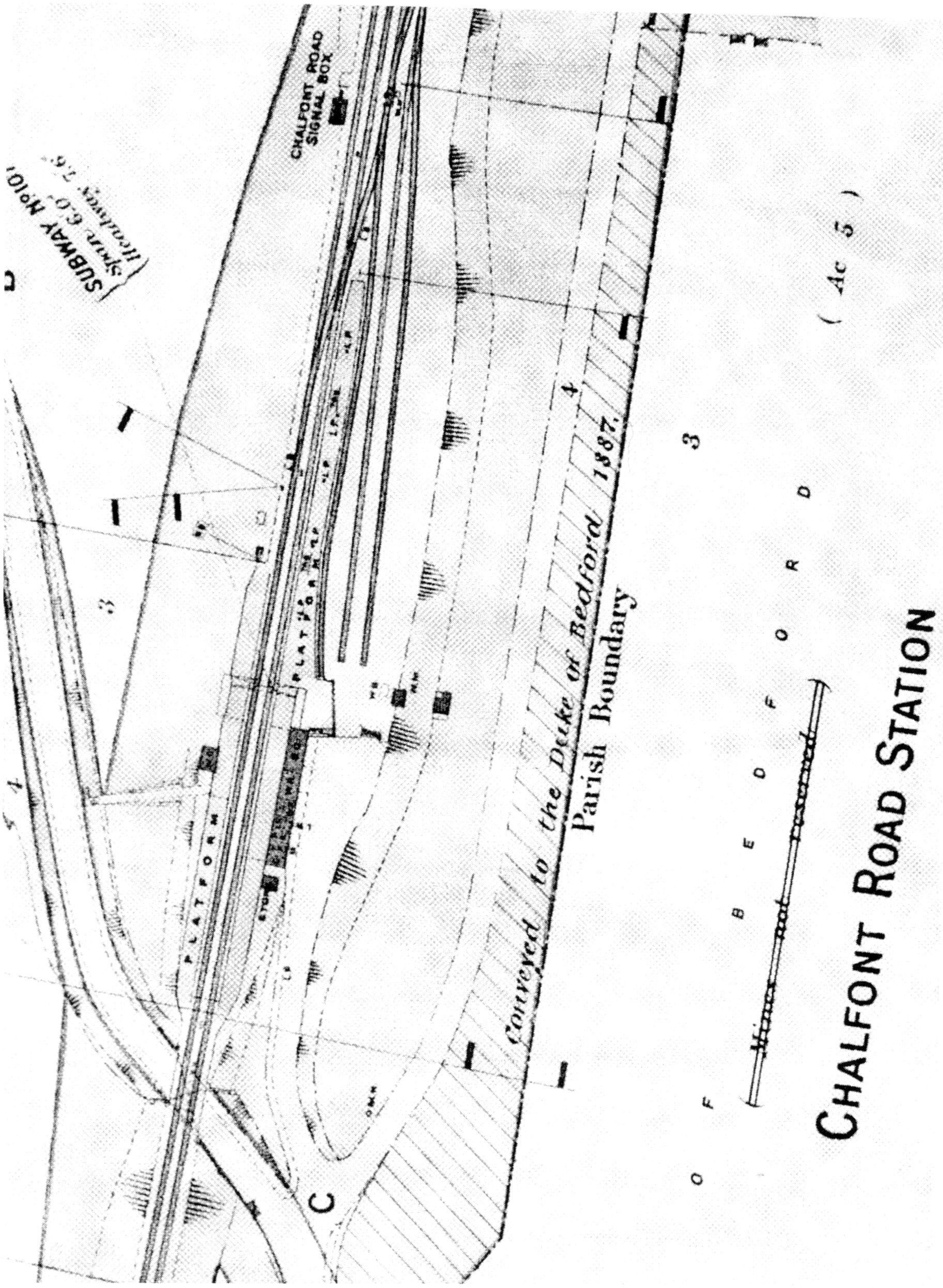

Chalfont was another of the Met stations that had connections between platforms via a subway which, thenceforth, going north was undertaken using bridges.
John Mock Collection

Entrance roads to Chalfont & Latimer Station in 1934, note right of station building entrance to goods yard. A tall signal with repeater arm on the 'up' side, this would allow long distance sighting and visibility in case of fog. Note also the long brick industrial building on the other side of the bridge adjoining the 'down' side platform. It appeared just after the first world war when the motor car period began to develop in earnest. It is a garage now and judging by the sign on the side that advertises 'Armstrong Siddeley' the motor car manufacturer, that is what it was then. The name alongside that is 'Graham', whether this is a trade name or the name of the original owner is not known. Perhaps it had associations with one of the many small firms that ran charabanc trips from stations in the Chilterns. The road going under the bridge is the A404 that passes through the town and is a great deal busier now than it appears here.

London's Transport Museum

Through train from Chesham the 10.04 leaving Chalfont in 1933 behind 'H' class 4-4-4T no 108.

R K Blencowe

Bracket platform starter for main line and branch to Chesham at Chalfont. In bay Chesham train stock and beyond are the goods sidings.

H C Casserley

Engine 67416 C13 4-4-2T originally a Great Central Railway locomotive working out its final days from Neasden shed. In this view it has just brought 1.30 pm train from Liverpool Street to Chesham Saturdays only on the 23 of July 1955.

H C Casserley

The LNER absorbing the GCR took up their interests on the Joint Committee, consequently LNER locomotives appear on trains formerly operated by the GCR. Here L1 2-6-4T 67794 brings the 9.14 am Aylesbury to Baker Street into Chalfont on the 23 of July, 1955. Originally numbered from 9000, the new 2-6-4T L1 was the first design at the end of the war in Europe in 1945. A novel feature at the time were electric lights front and tail and in the cab. They had a tractive effort of 32,000lb, the highest in the country for an engine of this type. In 1945 the LNER announced plans to construct another 1000 locomotives.

H C Casserley

H C Casserley

Chalfont on the 23 July, 1955, C13 no 67418 brings in the Chesham shuttle to the bay platform.

Ex Met tank 0-4-4T L44 at Chalfont & Latimer on August 12, 1951.

John H Meredith

Earlier view of E class no 80 on the Chesham shuttle in Metropolitan days, the locomotive was scrapped in 1941.

RAS Marketing

The shuttle in the murky days of January 1959.

H C Casserley

Looking south at Chalfont & Latimer May 10, 1977 the goods yard has now become a car park.

N D Munday

Engine L48 on a rambler's excursion called the John Milton Special at Chalfont on June 3, 1956. This special train ran from New Cross in south east London to the Chiltern Hills, L48 worked it from Rickmansworth.

R M Casserley

An Aylesbury train near Chalfont from Liverpool Street July 23, 1955.

H C Casserley

The Chesham branch push-pull approaching Chalfont behind C13 4-4-0T no 67418 on May 1956.
RAS Marketing

Chapter Five

Chesham

The promotion of a railway to Chesham by the Metropolitan was met with some consternation by the people of the town, when it was realised that the railway planned to terminate in Mill Field, half a mile from the town centre. In reaction to this four prominent townsmen, Mr W Lowndes, Mr J W Reading, E Reynolds and G W Webb expressed their concern. They were instrumental in securing financial support, over £2,000, to have the railway extended to a position taken along the back, parallel with and to the north end of the High Street, with a large goods shed close by Nash's Brewery.

The first passenger train to pass along the branch was on May 10, 1889 on that day at 11.45 am a train with the chairman and directors acompanied by a multitude of greater or lesser participants left Baker Street for Rickmansworth where they were joined by another party from Chesham which had been a slow journey as the new line had not yet been passed for public traffic. The combined assemblage proceeded back to Chesham where the station was decorated for the event.

Baron Ferdinand Rothschild, MP spoke to the assemblage in the goods shed which had been prepared with a cold luncheon. Guests included the ever present Chairman of the Metropolitan Railway Sir Edward Watkin, MP and the General Manager, John Bell. A toast was proclaimed to the Queen and the memory of the late Duke of Buckingham who had been a railway Duke, being chairman of the Aylesbury & Buckingham and London & North Western Railways, plus a tramway of his own to Brill, the Wotton Tramway.

As Chairman Watkin spoke of the desire of George Stephenson over fifty years ago to see the first main line railway pass the way of the Metropolitan. At that time it had been affected against by various antagonists of the locality. Tactfully he did not mention that the first Duke of Buckingham at Stowe had been a vociferous opponent of the London & Birmingham Railway. There was some tongue in cheek joking that it was hoped that a sudden influx of cockneys would not oust the grazing sheep with the access to London. Many a true word said in jest, as a more populous Chilterns was what the esteemed chairman was after, although it would not be cockneys that would be able to take advantage of this new arcadia. He congratulated the inhabitants on the choice of the station location (at their cost) and that the goods shed in which they stood would soon be filled with all manner of merchandise that had, hitherto, cost five shillings a ton to reach the nearest railhead. He also mentions that sure prosperity would increase, especially if they went on to Tring. Watkin was publicly admitting that he hoped for a Tring connection. Quite clearly the LNWR did not!

An interesting reference is made by the London correspondent of the *Birmingham Post* who wrote that the the line to Aylesbury was planned to meet the Worcester & Broom Railway to make a connection to Birmingham and become a rival to the North Western. One can imagine that on reading that news the board of the LNWR would be likely to say 'over our prostrate corpses it will!'.

That as it may, the good townspeople of Chesham became officially connected by rail of nearly twenty-six miles to the capital on Monday July 8, 1889 when 1,500 sated their curiosity to travel on the line. Tuesday would see 600, 300 of which booked to go to the Crystal Palace, the splendour of which they would only have known of by word or illustrated engravings.

It would be another three years before the hilly route on to Aylesbury would be completed and for the Met that would be the high point of their achievement. A little further brought connection with the GCR, but after that it was a diminishing prospect, tailing away to Verney Junction.

The Chesham branch was formerly worked by electric tablet, but in 1949 the single line was track circuited and colour light co-acting signals installed. This enabled the branch to be worked without token, the signals at one end automatically locking with those at the other end of the line.

Notification appeared in the press in 1936 that the LPTB were planning to electrify the four miles from Chalfont to Chesham but as this had to be in negotiation with their erstwhile partners the LNER, the LT stated that this was premature. They claimed that in July they had ordered two 260 bhp diesel engine AEC streamlined railcars to run the branch.

In October 1952 a new diesel train ran on the Chalfont - Chesham shuttle with diesel engines like Greenline buses, in fact it looked just like a bus. It was on test for a fortnight from the maker Commercial Vehicles of Southall. It was received as a great novelty driven from each end and crowded with curious passengers. It had a two tone klaxon. The railwaymen were apprehensive for their jobs, with good reason, but not with this vehicle. In all probability it suffered the fate of all vehicles tested on tracks with bus panelling intended for pneumatic tyres, unpleasant vibration. This was a problem for early diesel multiple units designed for the railway.

Neverthless the economics of the tests, all around the Chilterns, would not be lost on the operating department.

Electric trains ran to Chesham first of all on August 15, 1960 using multiple unit 'T' stock and with some trains electric locomotive hauled using the Aylesbury stock, these could use the run-round at Chesham.

The introduction of the service came on September 12, 1960. Peak trains to Baker Street were electric locomotive hauled whilst the Chesham-Chalfont shuttle was operated by three-car electric sets, the introduction of electricity to Amersham allowed an extra twenty trains per day.

The last days of the steam shuttle were September 11. On the day before an historic moment was repeated from all those years ago, when Sir Edward Watkin had regailed the townsmen with advantages of the new railway. Descendants of the same townsmen who had attended that meeting boarded the final steam shuttle to Chalfont and back. Councillor Baines hung a wreath on the engine which was specially rostered by British Railways. Remarkably a Mr Albert Wilcox, who was aged eighty-six, had also seen the line open. After the platform eulogies all repaired to the Council Chamber for a special reception, doubtless to toast, with a lament to the old steam service, and to bring in the new power of electricity.

Important rail developed industries at Chesham were leather tanning, wood for furniture and brushes and considerable watercress traffic.

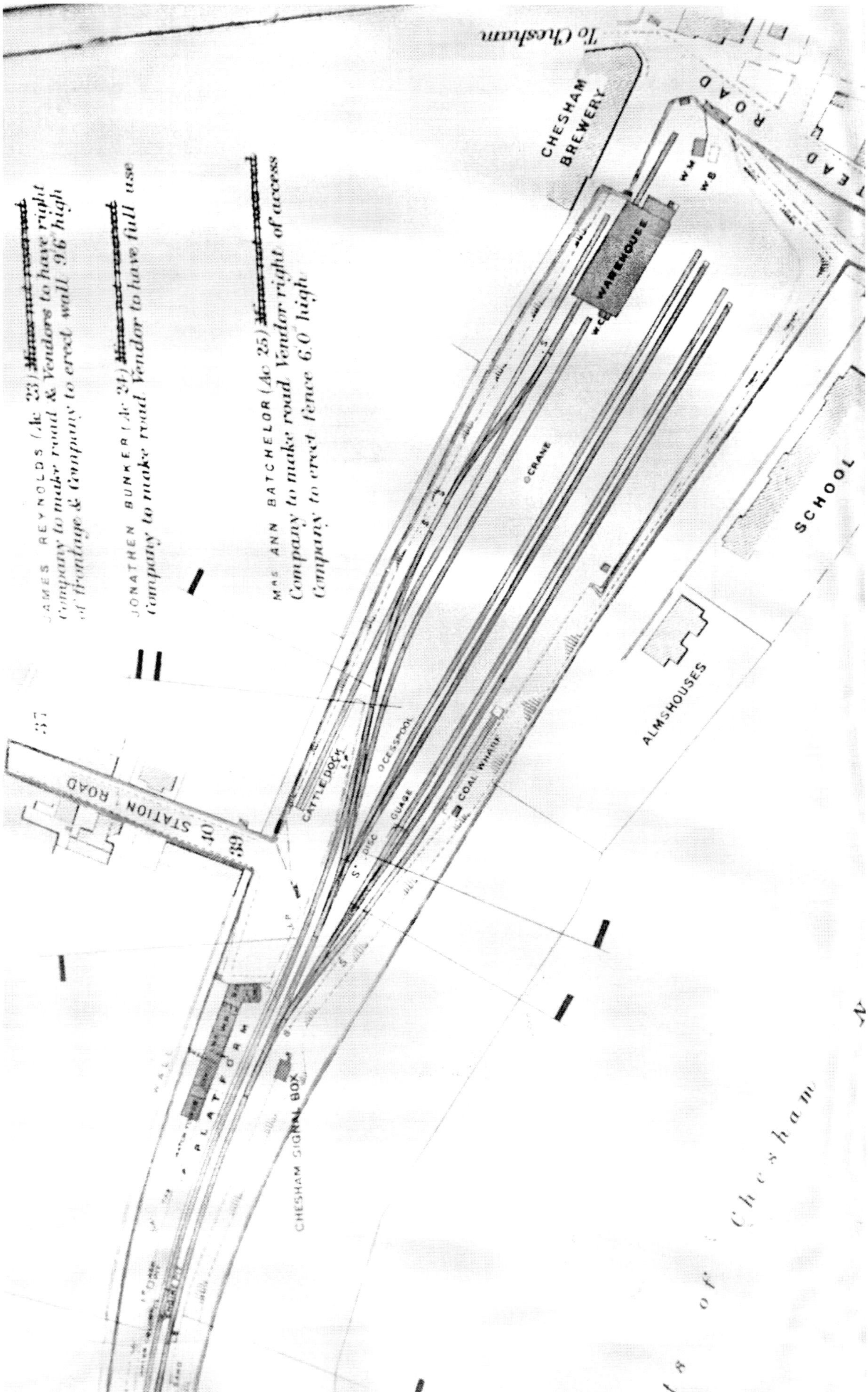

Station and terminus of Chesham in 1908. Goods services on the Metropolitan up until 1933 were operated by the Joint Committee. After that time goods trains continued to be hauled by London Transport locomotives until 1937. From that time the large tank engines that handled goods were sold to the LNER who continued operating the goods service with them.
John Mock Collection

A Superb study of the branch train at Chesham in 1951. Note distant locomotive on line of turntable, which was probably used by tender GCR engines working goods trains to Chesham.
Alan Willmott

The approach to Chesham station in 1934. Note the Metropolitan style shaded lettering on the signalbox, an uncommon detail compared to other railway companies.
London's Transport Museum

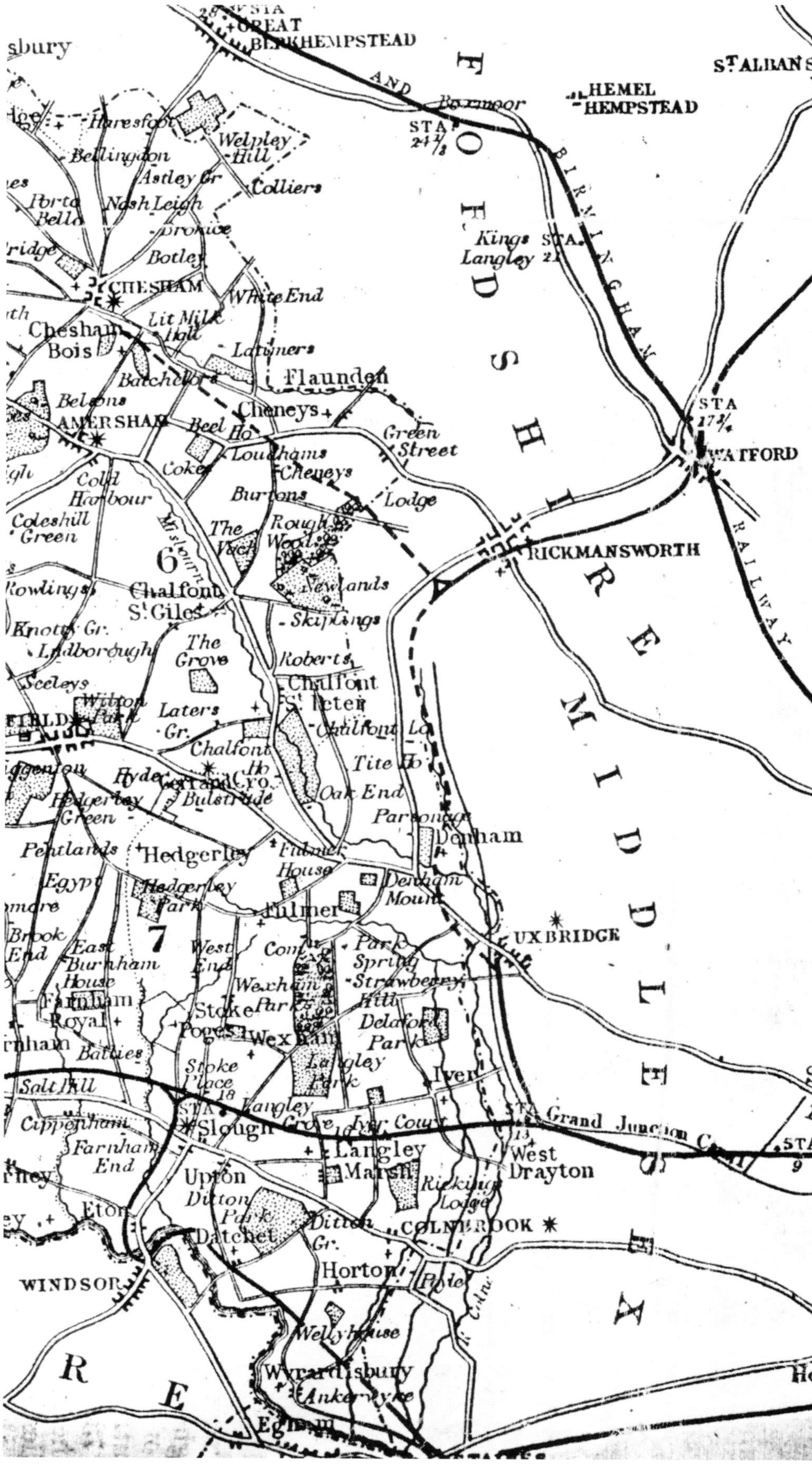

Between the London & Birmingham line top right and the Great Western main line below left an independent proposal in 1863 to connect both and give them both access to Chesham by extending the Rickmansworth and Uxbridge branches. An ambitious plan that failed to generate support.

The branch train with its C13 4-4-0T here crossing Moor Road at Waterside near Chesham in the summer of 1955. A time far removed, when one could take leisurely stroll down the middle of the road!

Alan Willmott

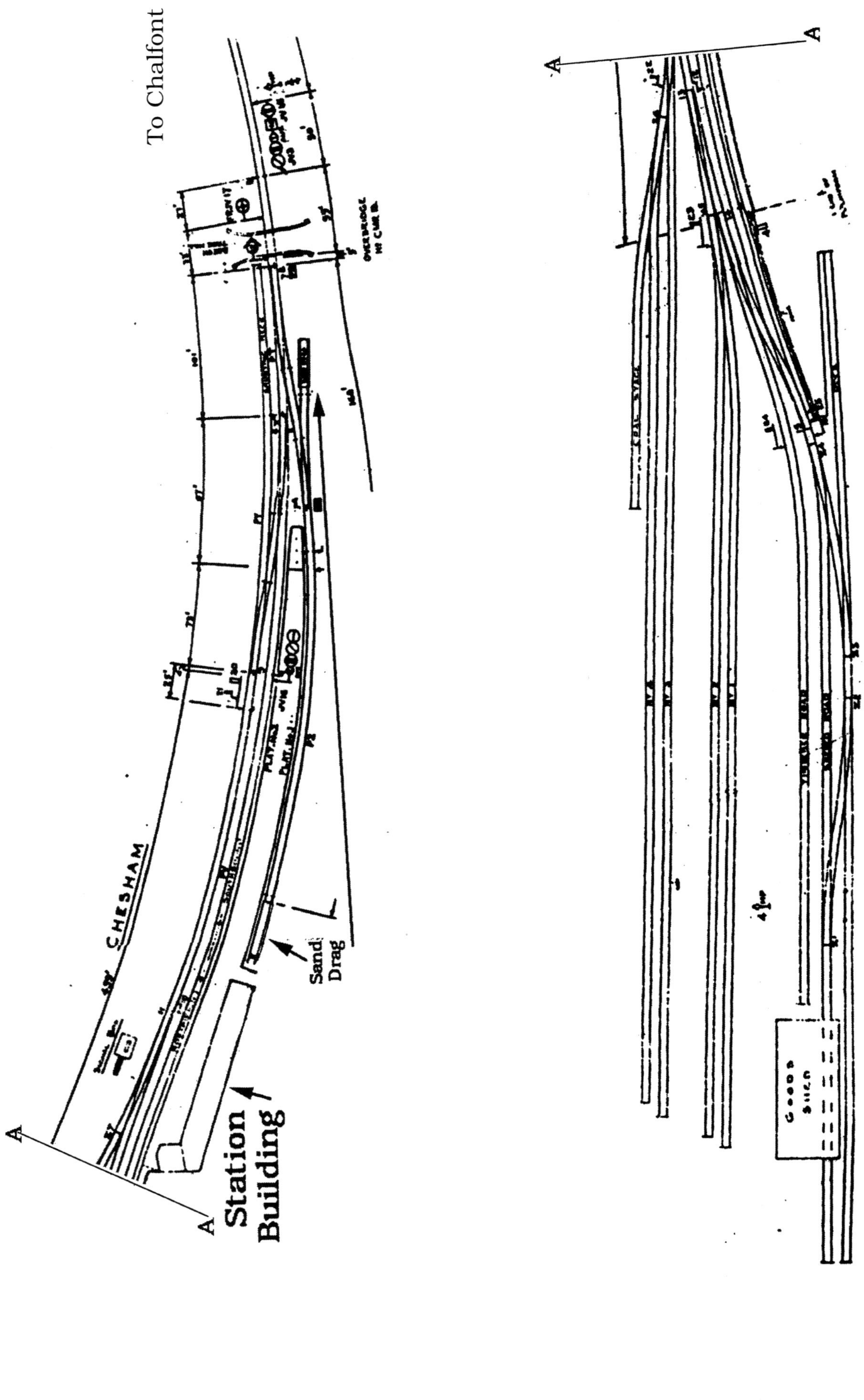

These drawings supplied and created by Mike Crosbie

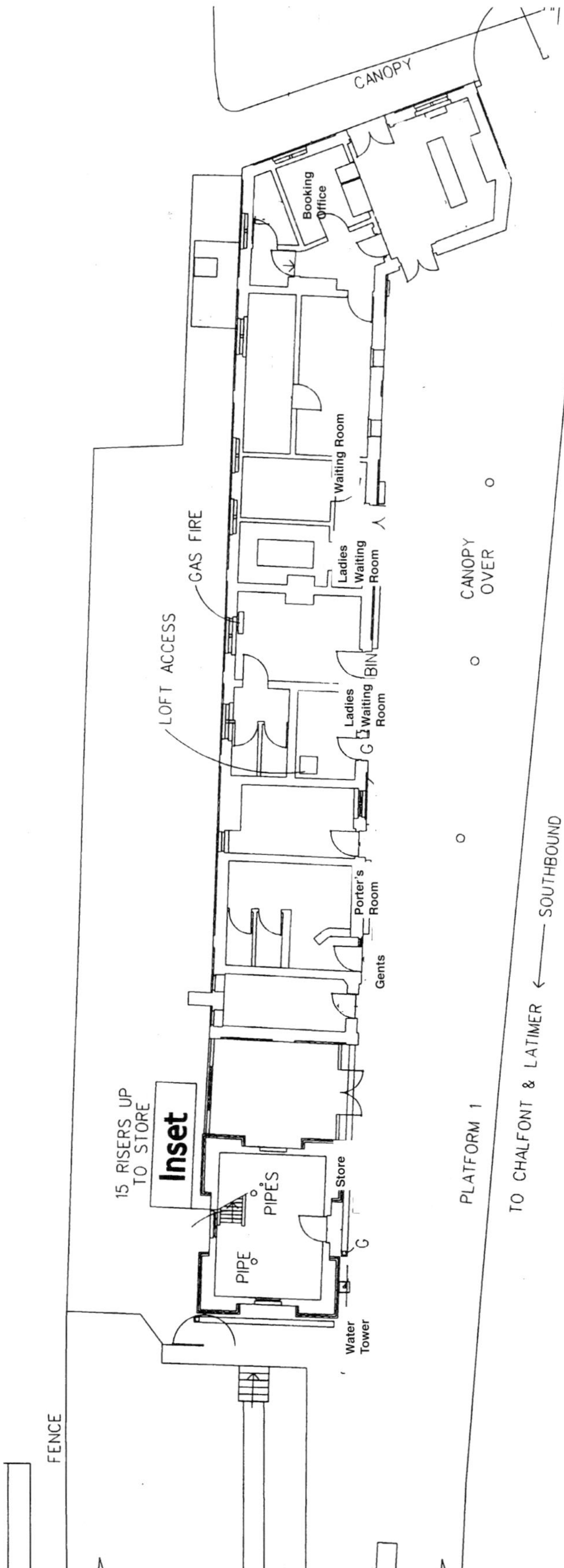

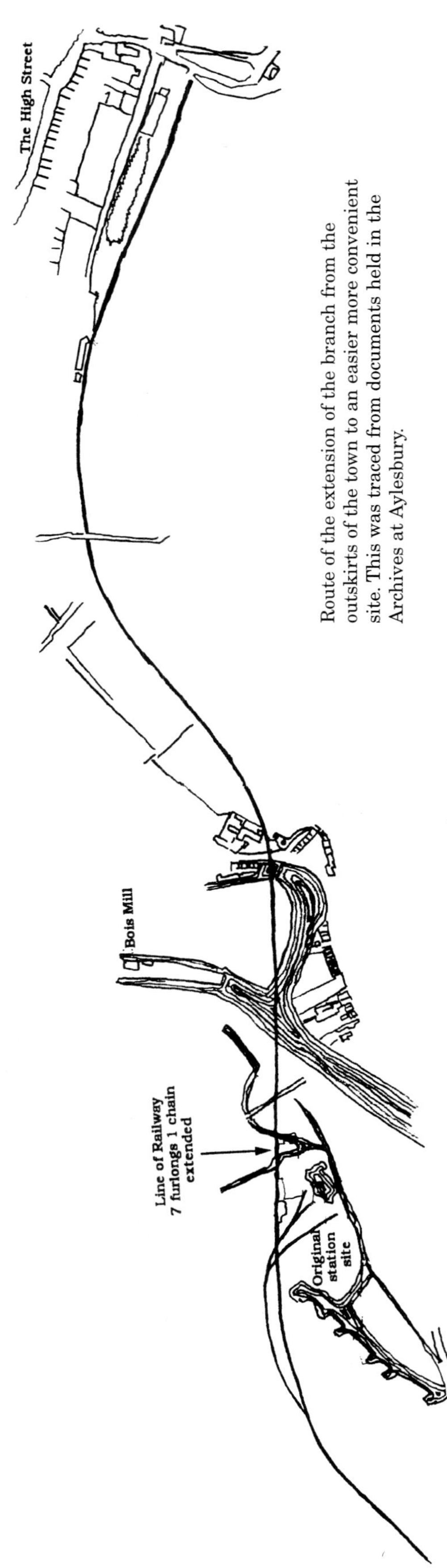

Route of the extension of the branch from the outskirts of the town to an easier more convenient site. This was traced from documents held in the Archives at Aylesbury.

Affectionately regarded the steam shuttle ended its days with the arrival of electrification. Here local people assemble to say their goodbyes and welcome in the new electric trains represented here by T stock, in the summer of 1960.

London's Transport Museum

Evidently the last rites were undertaken by Ivatt 2-6-2T no 41284. Earlier, in the 1950's this engine had been at Skipton shed, a far cry from the exposed Pennine reaches to the wooded Chilterns.

London's Transport Museum

Patiently awaiting passengers the busy shuttle stands at Chesham station on 23 of July, 1955. Some shunting work is being undertaken by an L1.

H C Casserley

The goods yard at Chesham holding a significant number of coaches. Note the shuttle train in the distance.

Peter Waylett

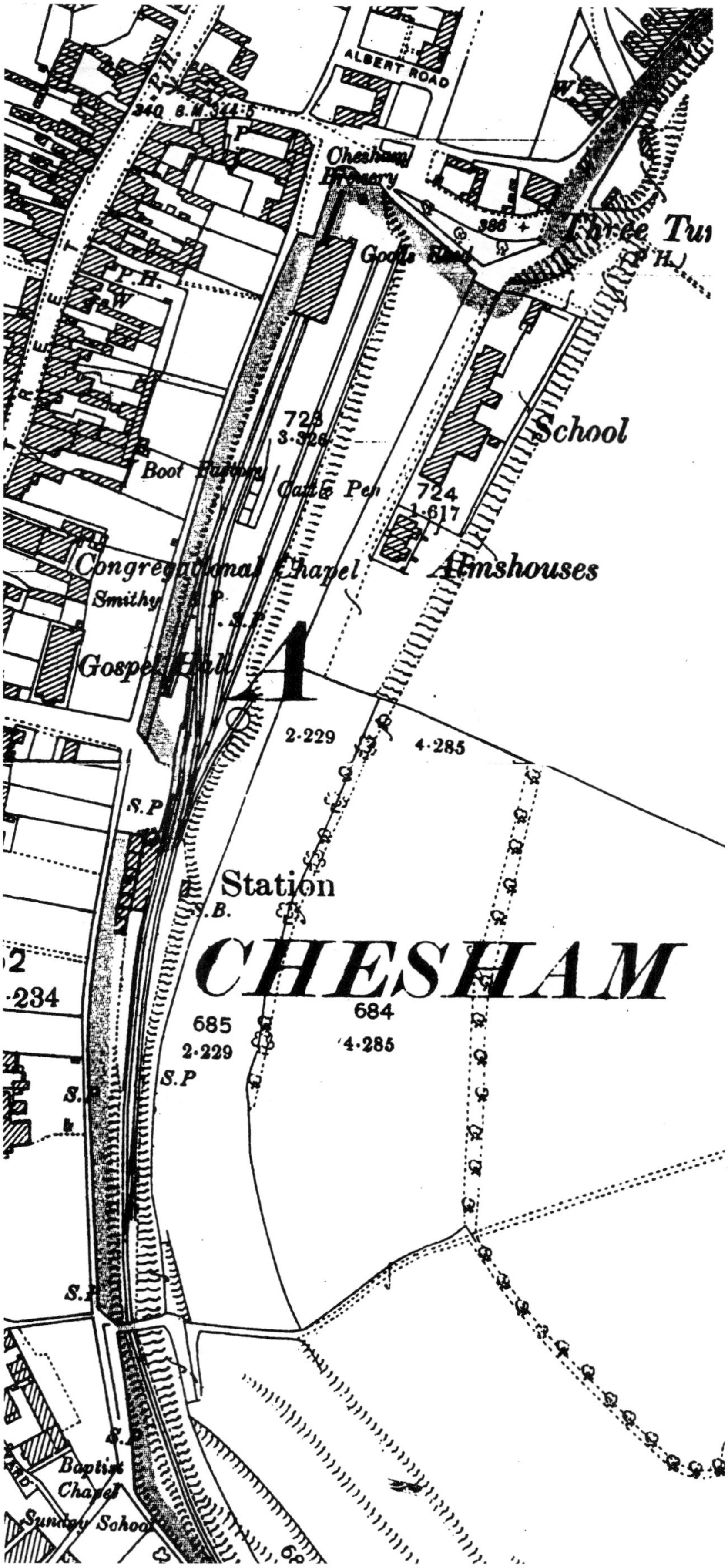

Survey of the location of the station in relation to the town, note turntable.

Ordnance Survey

Ivatt 2-6-2T no 41329 on the shuttle duty on January 3, 1959.

R M Casserley

Chesham station was the last site of Metropolitan signals seen here on April 26, 1953.

Mike Crosbie

Platform view January 3, 1959.

H C Casserley

Met coaches at Chesham no 445 and L48 with L44 0-4-4T on June 3, 1956.

R M Casserley

Train en route near Chesham with C13 4-4-0T 67418.

H C Casserley

METROPOLITAN RAILWAY.

CHESHAM BRANCH.

WEEK DAYS.

		A.M	A.M	A.M	A.M	A.M	A.M	A.M	P.M	P.M	P.M	P.M	P.M	P.M	P.M	P.M	P.M	P.M	P.M	P.M	P.M	P.M
CHESHAM	dep.	...	7 30	...	8 43	...	10 0	11 0	...	1 0	...	3 0	...	4‡ 0	5 0	...	...	7 0	8 0	9 0	10 0	...
Chalfont Road	,,	...	7 41	...	8 53	...	1011	1111	...	1 11	...	3 11	...	4‡11	5 11	...	...	7 11	8 11	9 11	1011	...
Chorley Wood	,,	...	7 45	...	8 57	...	1015	1115	...	1 15	...	3 15	...	4‡15	5 15	6*15	...	7 15	8 15	9 15	1015	...
Rickmansworth	,,	7 20	7 50	8 20	9 2	9 51	1020	1120	1220	1 20	2 20	3 20	3‡50	4 20	5 20	6 20	6 50	7 20	8 20	9 20	1020	1120
BAKER STREET	arr.	8 5	8 35	9 5	9 37	1035	11 5	12 5	1 5	2 5	3 5	4 5	4 35	5 5	6 5	7 5	7 35	8 5	9 5	10 5	11 5	12 5

		A.M	A.M	A.M	A.M	A.M	A.M	A.M	A.M	P.M	P.M	P.M	P.M	P.M	P.M	P.M	P.M	P.M	P.M	P.M	P.M	¶
BAKER STREET	dep.	6 19	6 49	7 29	8 29	9 4	9 29	1029	1129	1229	1 29	2‡27	3 29	4 29	5§27	5‡29	5 59	6 29	7 29	8 29	1029	1140
Rickmansworth	,,	7 3	7 36	8 13	9 13	9 45	1013	1113	1213	1 13	2 13	3‡ 5	4 13	5 13	6§ 3	6‡13	6 43	7 13	8 13	9 13	1113	1233
Chorley Wood	,,	7 8	...	8 19	9 19	...	1019	...	1219	...	2 19	3‡11	4 19	5*19	6§ 9	6‡19	...	7 19	8 19	9 19	...	1239
Chalfont Road	,,	7 13	...	8 24	9 24	...	1024	...	1224	...	2 24	3‡16	4 24	...	6§14	6‡24	...	7 24	8 24	9 24	...	1244
CHESHAM	arr.	7 23	...	8 34	9 34	...	1034	...	1234	...	2 34	3‡26	4 34	...	6§24	6‡34	...	7 34	8 34	9 34	...	1254

* Tuesdays, Thursdays, and Saturdays only. § Saturdays excepted. ‡ Saturdays only.
¶ Wednesdays only.

SUNDAYS.

		A.M	A.M	A.M	P.M	P.M	P.M	P.M	P.M	P.M	P.M	P.M	P.M	P.M	P.M	P.M	P.M	P.M
CHESHAM	dep.	...	...	9 59	1249	...	2 49	...	4 49	...	6 49	...	...	...	8 53	...	9 49	1029
Chalfont Road	,,	...	...	1010	1 0	...	3 0	...	5 0	...	7 0	...	...	...	9 4	...	10 0	1040
Chorley Wood	,,	...	...	1014	1 4	...	3 4	...	5 4	...	7 4	...	...	...	9 8	...	10 4	1044
Rickmansworth	,,	8 15	...	1019	1 9	2 9	3 9	4 9	5 9	6 9	7 9	7 39	8 13	8 39	9 13	9 39	10 9	1049
BAKER STREET	arr.	9 0	...	11 4	1 54	2 54	3 54	4 54	5 54	6 54	7 54	8 24	8 58	9 24	9 58	1024	1054	...

		A.M	A.M	A.M	A.M	A.M	A.M	P.M	P.M	P.M	P.M	P.M	P.M	P.M	P.M	P.M	P.M	P.M
BAKER STREET	dep.	...	8 47	...	9 47	1047	...	1 16	2 16	3 16	4 16	5 16	6 16	6 46	7 16	7 46	8 16	9 16
Rickmansworth	,,	...	9 30	...	1030	1130	...	2 0	3 0	4 0	5 0	6 0	7 0	7 30	8 0	8 30	9 0	10 0
Chorley Wood	,,	...	9 35	...	1036	...	...	2 6	...	4 6	...	6 6	...	...	8 6	...	9 6	10 6
Chalfont Road	,,	...	9 40	...	1041	...	...	2 11	...	4 11	...	6 11	...	...	8 11	...	9 11	1011
CHESHAM	arr.	...	9 50	...	1051	...	...	2 21	...	4 21	...	6 21	...	...	8 21	...	9 21	1021

Timetable for the Chesham branch on April 30, 1892

Bill Simpson Collection

Engine 0-4-4T L48 at Chesham on the 'John Milton Special' on June 3, 1956

R M Casserley

The shuttle near Chalfont with 67418 on July 23, 1955.

H C Casserley

In Arcadia, the branch line train waits for special custom.

Peter Waylett

Hot box!, concerned discussion at the lineside for L.48 running a special on the branch in the fifties.

Peter Waylett

The shuttle seen from the field side.

Peter Waylett

Leaving Chesham, a few days before the end of steam services.

Peter Waylett

Driver Ted Copperwaite talks to a lady porter, Mrs Nellie Dean, at Chalfont and Latimer station in October 1952. More correctly described as a railbus, this was an early post war experiment of an alternative to steam traction. Supplied by (ACV) Commercial Vehicles of Southall. The train was described as having three coaches with their motors mounted under the floors, so it would be driven from both ends, like a diesel multiple unit. Like the early dmu's it almost certainly would have suffered from vibration problems.

Bucks Advertiser

The ACV experimental three-car lightweight diesel train at St Albans Abbey station during the summer of 1952. It enjoyed quite a diagram of movements on lines north of London during this summer.

T H Watts courtesy Railway Magazine

Ivatt 2-6-2T 41284 on the last day of steam September 11, 1960 suitably wreathed.

N D Munday

A fine study of the Metropolitan design signalbox on September 10, 1960 that remains still, but is totally disused.

London Underground Railway Society/H Clarke

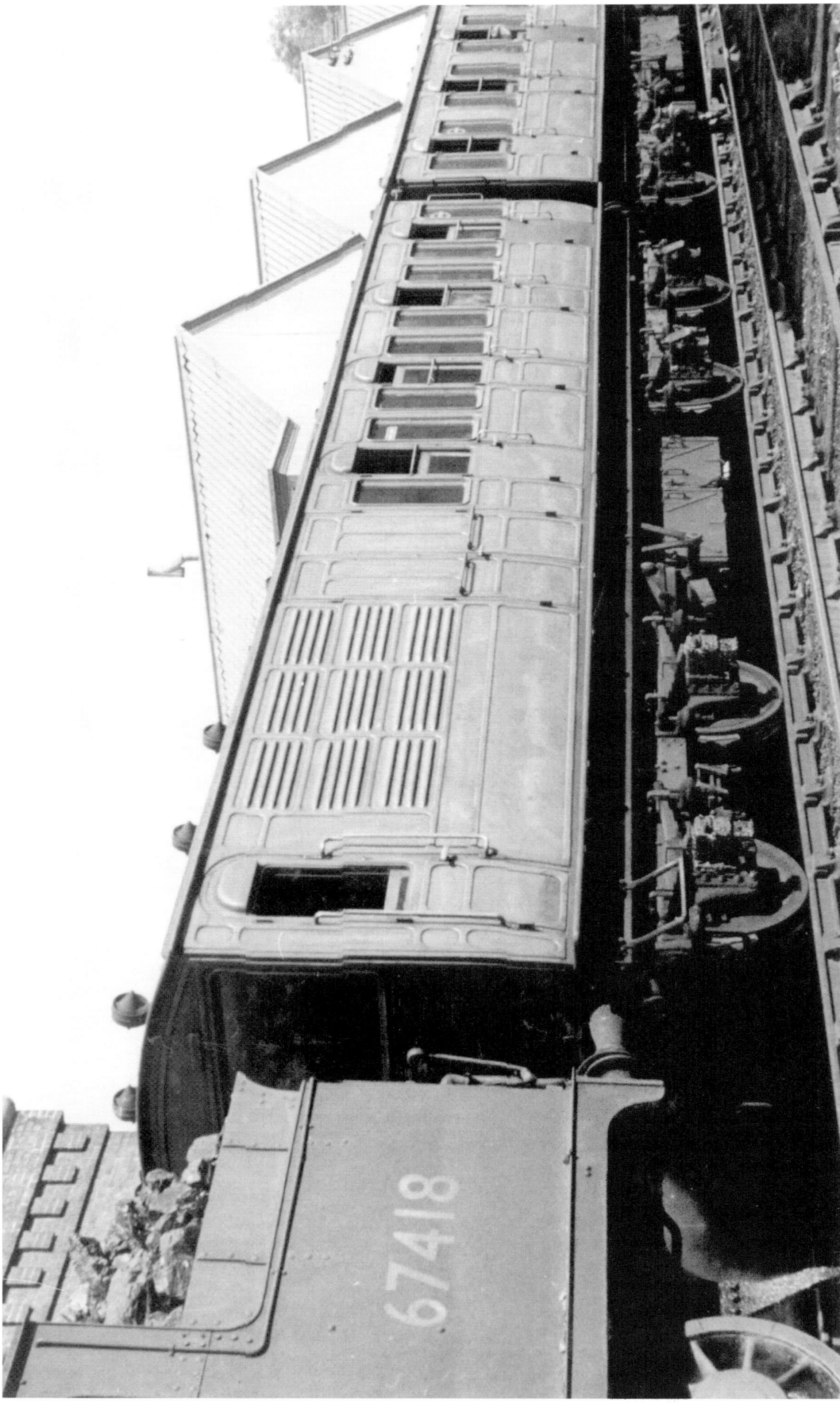

Brake of Chesham branch set coach no 513 in July 1955.

H C Casserley

Amersham station c 1948 with H class tank entering.

Alan Willmott

Chapter Six

Amersham

In the final survey for the line the Amersham station which opened on September 1, 1892 was least favoured. The town of Amersham, now called Old Amersham is situated on the low land. But to avoid tunnelling the survey had to take high ground at this point. The railway then had to build a road to the station, which in the days of horse power would have been a trying business for ascending and descending. Consequently the later settlement of Amersham-on-the-Hill brought many businessess near to the railway and settled more conveniently where a new township would develop.

The Metropolitan Country Estates purchased the Weller Estate of 78 acres in 1930 to cover it in 535 semi-detached houses and 51 shops, the nucleus of the new Amersham.

On August 15, 1960 the overdue electrification of the line to Amersham was completed and opened for service. This would emphasise the consolidation of London Transport to a final terminus for their passenger services and effectively to terminate what had been the north extension of the Metropolitan. After the next six years their erstwhile partner in this, formerly the GCR, would see their hard wrought London Extension north closed and removed, but for a section between Quainton Road and Claydon on the Oxford and Bletchley line. In recent years some proposals have been made to replace it in view of the completed Channel Tunnel railway. Perhaps the restless spirit of Watkin is reincarnated in retribution to see this task at last fulfilled!

Signalling on the Line

For this section I am indebted to former signalman Tim Stevens

'With the introduction of the Joint Committee and block sections, signal cabins north from

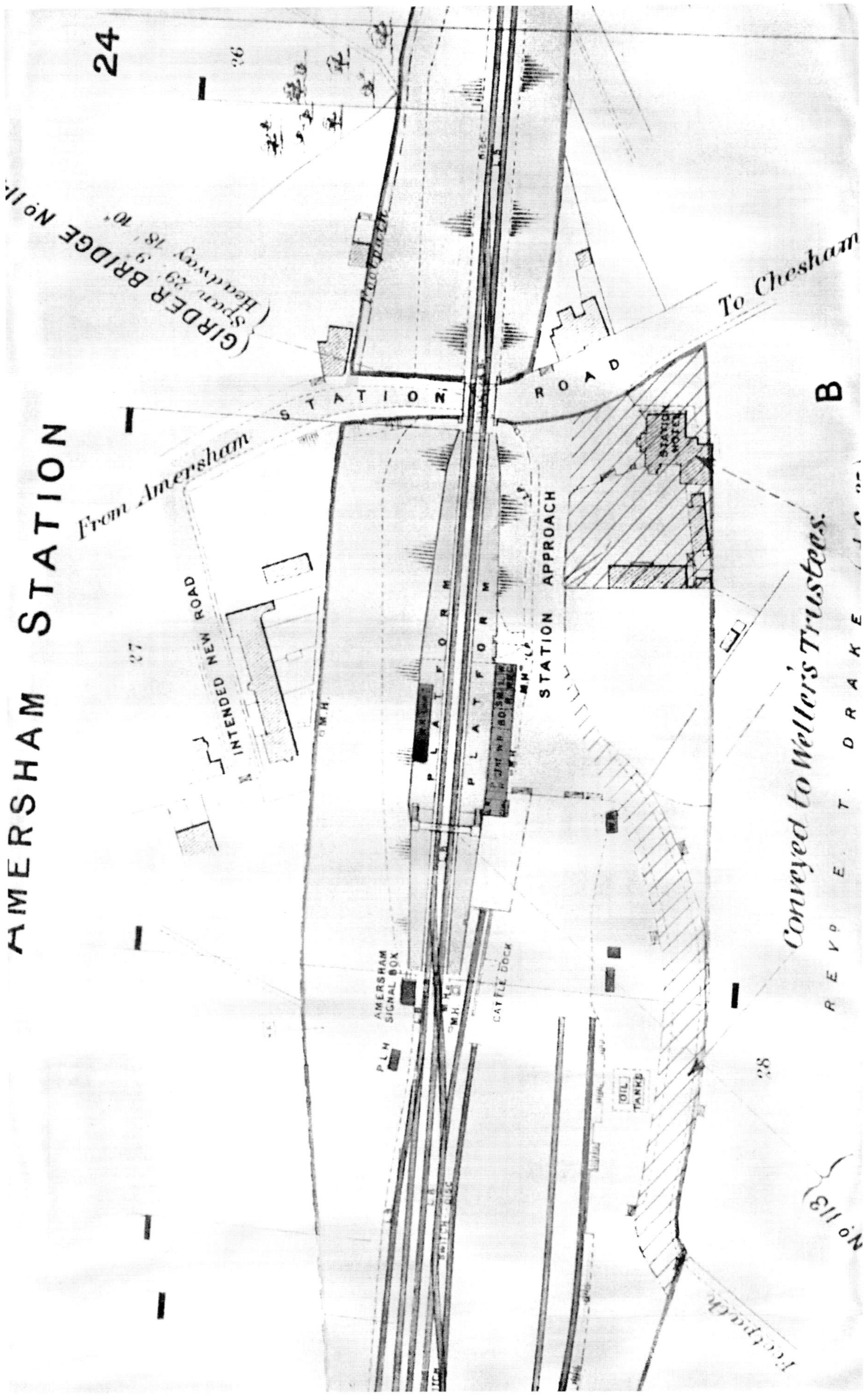

Amersham station on the hill. Note, the entrance to the goods yard that was once close by.

John Mock Collection.

One of the E class 0-4-4T on a Met train including a Pullman which would have been the Pullman service between the City and Verney Junction in 1910.

Railway Magazine

Amersham on the Metropolitan & Great Central Joint Railway were Amersham, Mantles Wood, Great Missenden, Dutchlands, Wendover and Stoke Mandeville. These were ordinary block posts for 'up' and 'down' lines. Later intermediate block semaphore signals were provided at Mantles Wood and at Dutchlands and the signal cabins closed and dismantled. These were replaced by colour light signals, including Stoke Mandeville. The signal cabin at the latter place was retained to work the points into the sidings. The colour light signals at Mantles Wood, between Amersham and Missenden were installed by LT at some time, probably as replacements for electrically worked intermediate semaphore signals Missenden no 5 'up' line; Amersham no 24 'down' line. Likely replacements for a signal box at Mantles Wood.

In 1960 full track circuiting was installed, between Amersham and Missenden on both lines, in conjunction with the comissioning of the new Amersham cabin. The control of Mantles Wood signals was altered; the 'up' line signals became automatic (A983/R983) and the 'down' line signals became Gt Missenden 30/R30.'

Maintenance between the LT and BR division was for the former to extend as far as $28^1/_2$ milepost, just south of Great Missenden.

'In 1984 these signals were removed and the track circuiting was abolished, working to standard Absolute Block. Although this seems a

Amersham that is now called Old Amersham where the line of railway was intended to go on the survey of 1845, an extension from the Buckinghamshire Railway. The alignment of the Metropolitan Railway, to avoid tunnels carried their alignment up on the hill.

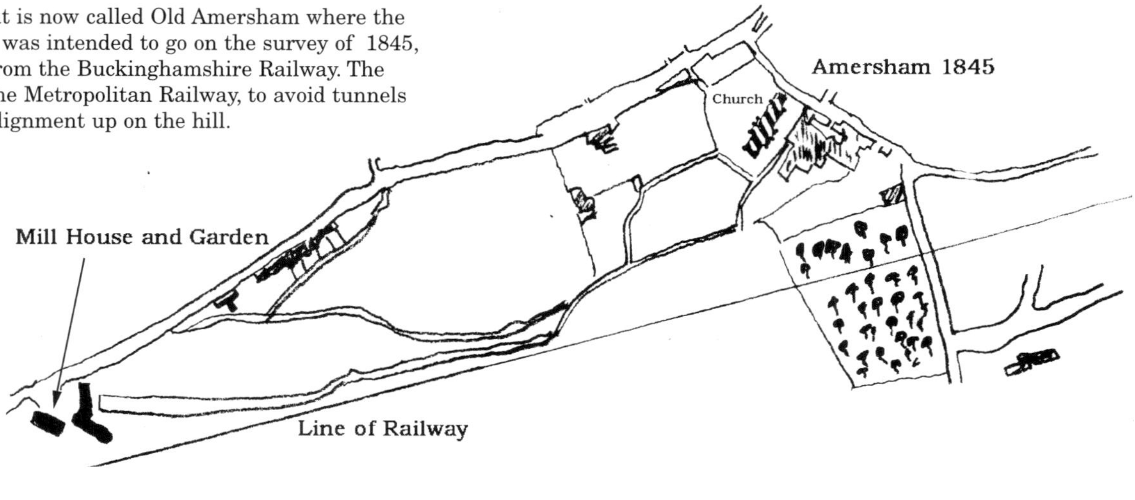

One of the G class 0-6-4T at Amersham on a train to Baker Street, with the name 'Lord Aberconway' he was a director of the Metropolitan. They had comparatively short lives due to being sold off to the LNER to whom they were outside the standard products of Doncaster and Darlington. This locomotive was introduced in 1915 and was withdrawn in 1937.

R K Blencowe / Lens of Sutton

retrograde step, I understand one of the reasons was the tendency for trains to disappear from track circuits during the leaf fall season, due to mulch on the rails. This was a potentially unsafe situation, because a signal could falsely go to 'green' because the track circuit showed 'clear' even though there was a train on it. Indeed, we had an instruction at Gt Missenden in the event of this occurring 'emergency block working' had to be instituted, using the train describer bell. This meant that a second train could not be allowed to leave Gt Missenden until the first was confirmed to have arrived at Amersham.'

Tim Stevens adds a personal recollection to the signalling history. 'When I became signalman in 1978 the two boxes were shadows of their former selves. Wendover had no points at all, merely signals. Missenden had only a crossover (rarely used) and no sidings. Much of the signalling was standard BR (LMR) upper quadrant, with modern BR block instruments, however, there were some relics of former LT and even some Met influence, such as Spagnoletti type block instruments at Wendover.

All this was swept away by the Marylebone resignalling of 1990 (computers and colour lights) although I believe the box at Missenden is still standing. Wendover box was dismantled in 1984 and the parts moved to Quainton Railway Centre.

Although I am not a signalling engineer, I understand some of the track circuits particularly between Missenden and Amersham were of the LT 'AC Vane Relay' type, rather than the conventional BR DC type. LT influence was also noticeable in the terminology, 'southbound' and 'northbound' instead of the usual 'up' and 'down', even after twenty years of British Rail!

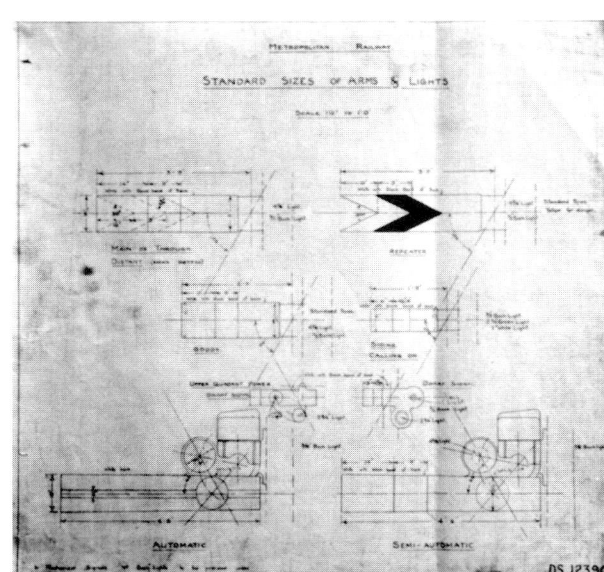

Details of Metropolitan Railway signals.

Mike Crosbie

A journey to stir the imagination, from the remote country station of Verney Junction at 8.50 am to the centre of the city at Liverpool Street. Handsomely headed by 'H' class 4-4-4 tank no 103 into Amersham & Chesham Bois on June 22, 1935.

H C Casserley

Aylesbury train near Amersham hauled by H class 4-4-4 tank no 110.

RAS Marketing

A Baker Street train about to leave Amersham in 1935 behind an 'H' class 4-4-4T no 107, later to become LNER H2 class no 6419. Note the three disc signal on the left which was for movements to and from the yard and 'down' siding, see detailed diagram on other page in this chapter After the second World War with advancing electrification to Amersham the 'down' platform became an island platform for extra tracks to allow for services beyond Amersham as LT services terminated there.

H C Casserley

Amersham goods yard August 17, 1959 with gas lit cattle dock. The wagon holds one of the early attempts of containerisation, heavy timber containers that could be craned from truck to wagon. The smallness of the wagon restricting the container size is self evidently a reason why this form of rail goods work required a drastic re-think to what we have today. The photograph below shows the predictable fate of the yard, a car park. Even this is now overbuilt and the entire area has been developed.

A J Reed

Engineer's Brake test train entering Amersham in the early seventies with electric stock being hauled by no 12 'Sarah Siddons' surviving representative of the class, now held in the London Transport Collection at Covent Garden. The dmu on the Marylebone train bottom left is in the new livery adopted in the this period in place of plain blue.

London Underground Railway Society

H C Casserley

Amersham & Chesham Bois with a more spectacular view along the track looking towards Aylesbury on June 22, 1935.

Amersham with new lines added and long footbridge, looking towards Aylesbury on March 25, 1961. Note on extreme left unelectrified goods loop, now removed.

H C Casserley

FAREWELL TO A STEAM TRAIN

A farewell to steam at Amersham as the electrified lines are extended from Rickmansworth and the British Railways diesel electric multiple units run a shuttle between Aylesbury and Amersham for Baker Street and continuing with all diesel on to Marylebone. About 500 enthusiasts crowded a five coach train and spectators crowded the platform at Amersham to see the last day. The engine was Fairburn 2-6-4T 42070, with driver D K Langstone and fireman F R Buckingham of Aylesbury shed.

Amersham looking south, in this view from January 1, 1959,

H C Casserley

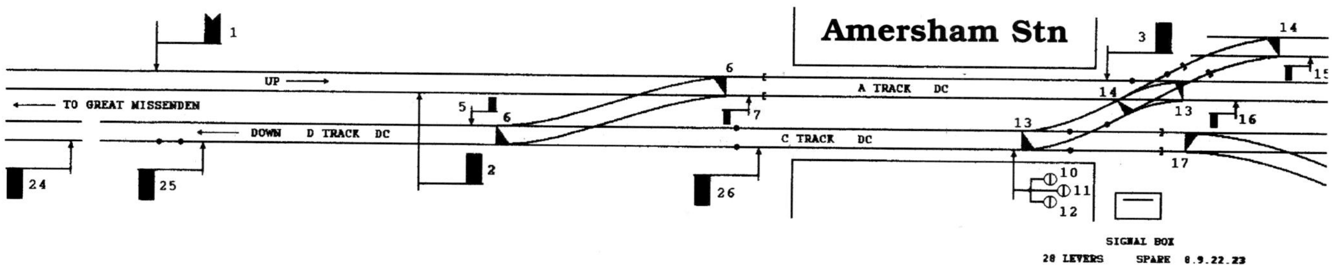

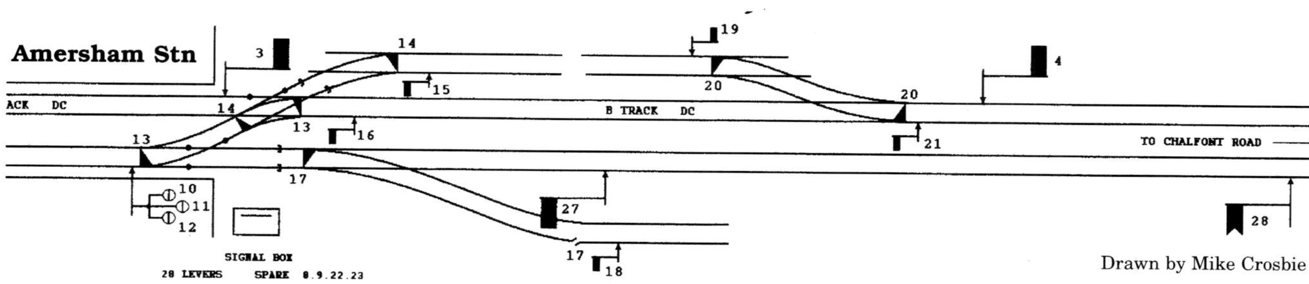

Drawn by Mike Crosbie

Movements controlled by the three direction signal on the platform at Amersham and other signalling.

1 up Distant
2 up Home
3 up starter
4 up Advance starter
5 Shunt down road to up platform 6
6 Crossover
7 Shunt up platform to down road 6
10 Shunt down platform to up siding 14
11 Shunt down platform to up road 13
12 Shunt down platform to down siding 17
13 Crossover
14 Crossover 13
15 Shunt up siding to down platform 14
16 Shunt up road to down platform 13
17 Crossover
18 Shunt down siding to down platform 17
19 Shunt up siding to up road 20
20 Crossover
21 Shunt up road to up siding 20
24 Down block to Great Missenden
25 Down advance starter
26 Down starter
27 Down home
28 Down distant

Metropolitan Railway Engineers Department Baker Street Station Drawing no SD2050 22.4.26

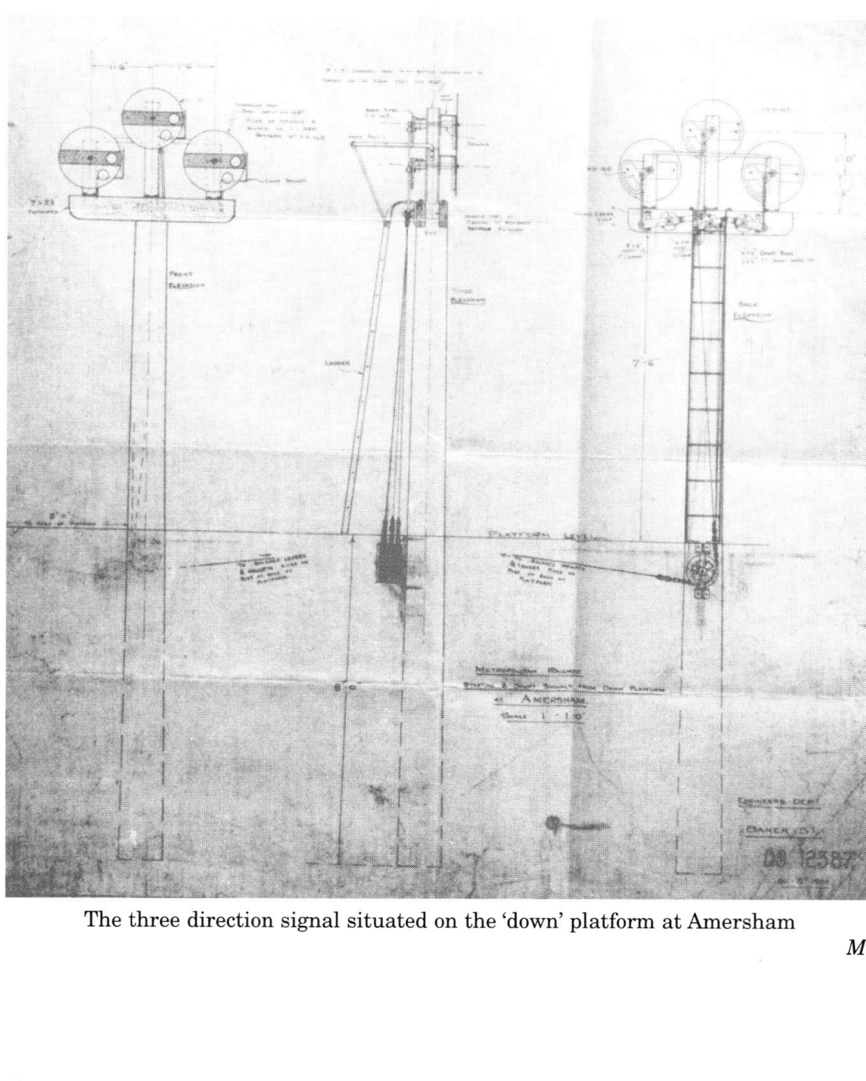

The three direction signal situated on the 'down' platform at Amersham

Mike Crosbie Collection

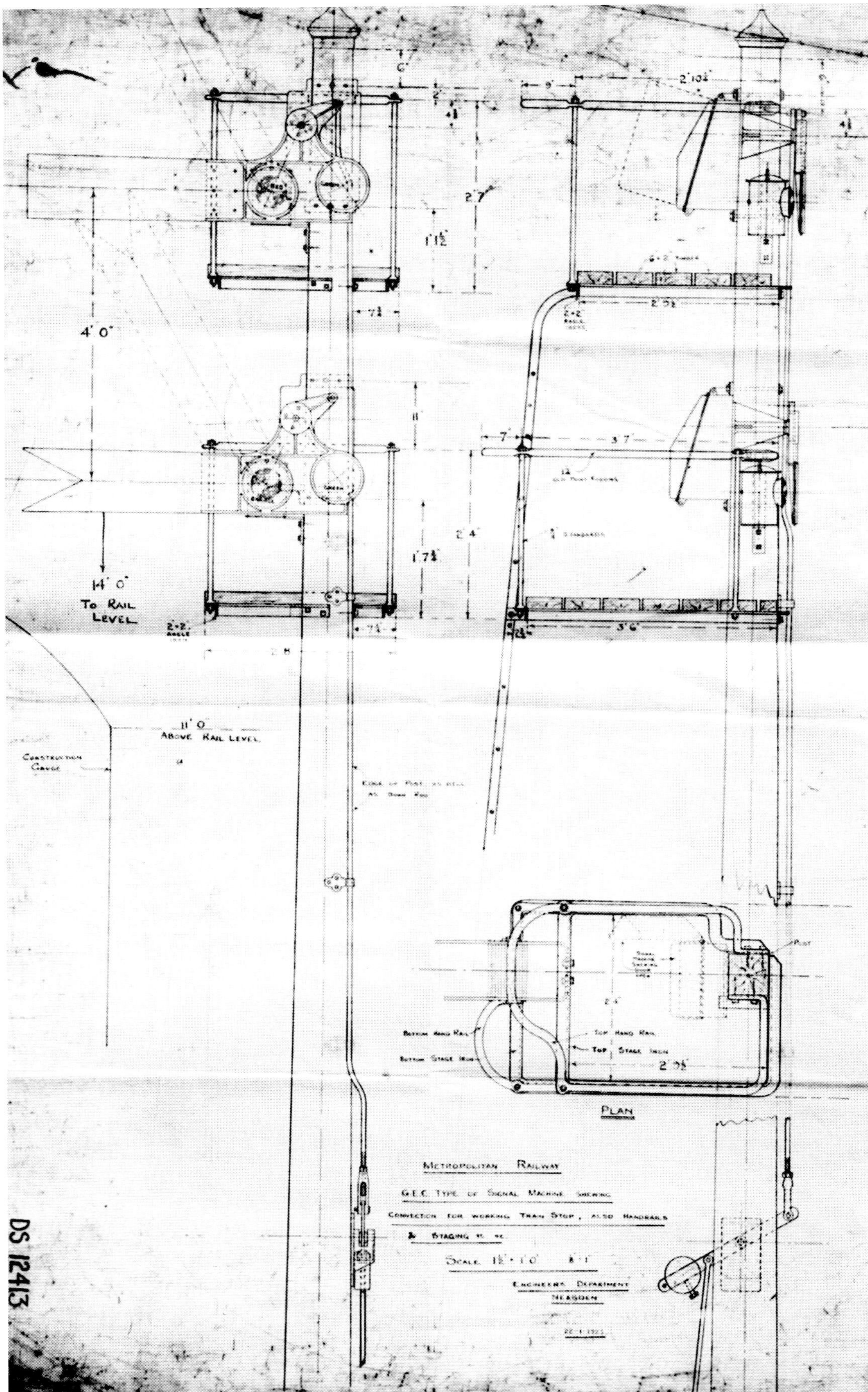

Drawings of the former signals used on the Met & GCR, Joint, now totally defunct. In an age that has mostly turned to electronic circuiting the simple mechanics almost achieve a kind of art form from the pre-electric age.

Mike Crosbie Collection

A train from Aylesbury entering Great Missenden in the 1930's. Buildings and platforms on the 'down' side were demolished in 1964.

H C Casserley

Chapter Seven

Great Missenden

At Great Missenden the country feel of the Metropolitan Chiltern line comes into its own. It was to places like this that the railway tempted new residents and weekend trippers. Coach companies advertising trips into the hills and carrier carts strung out their services from each of the stations. It caused no discord, like intensive road use would do sixty years later, but the area would never be quite the same again.

This was the hikers paradise, up from the city, a bracing day in the country and back to Harrow, Willesden Green or further. It became the celebrated image of the Metropolitan and London Transport in the poster art in twenties and thirties when there was such a splendid flowering of this medium.

Connections between countryside and city, an 'up' Met train hauled by Fowler 2-6-4T no 42338 from Aylesbury leaving Great Missenden for Liverpool Street on May 10, 1958.

H C Casserley

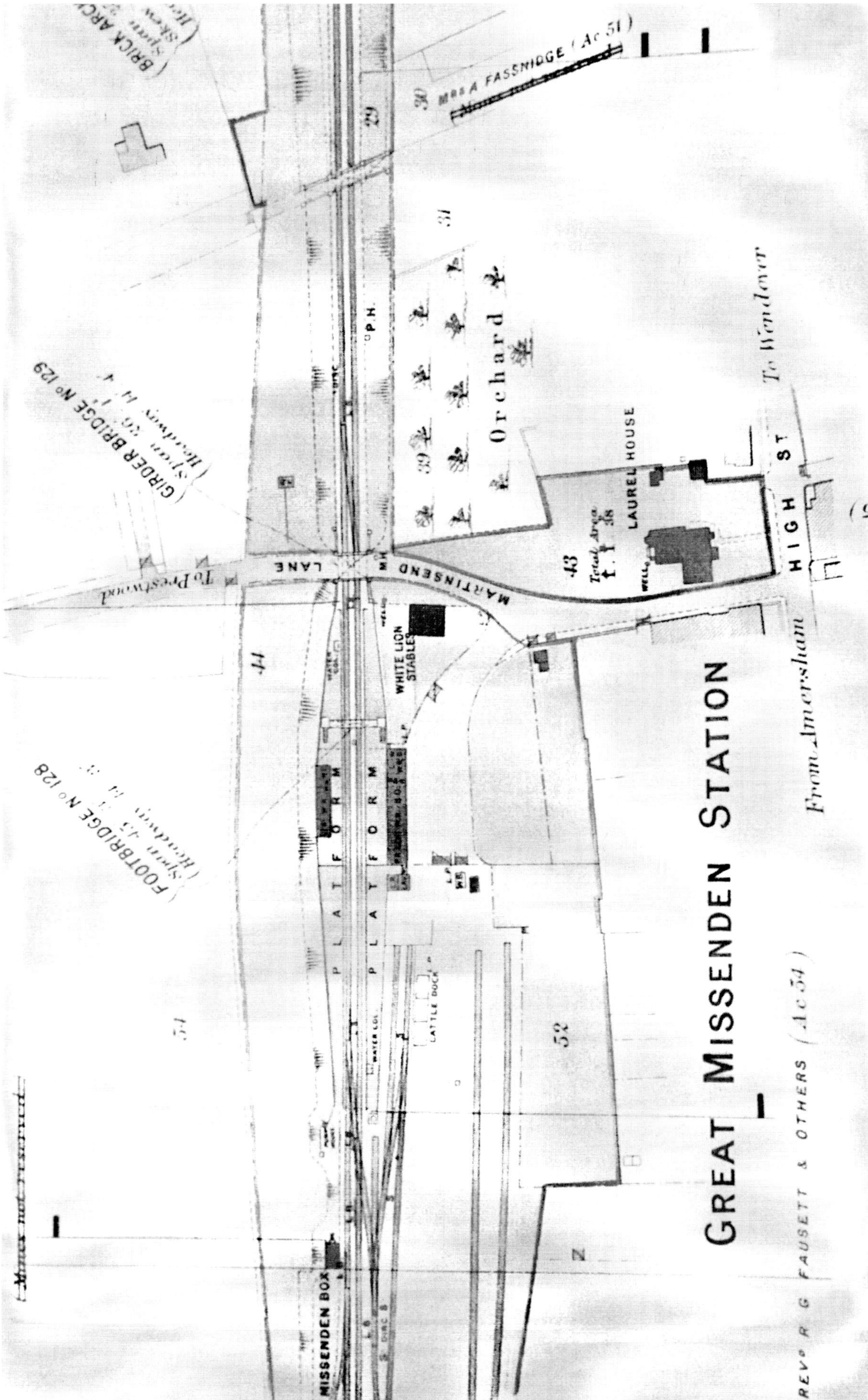

Ground plan of Great Missenden station in 1908.

John Mock Collection

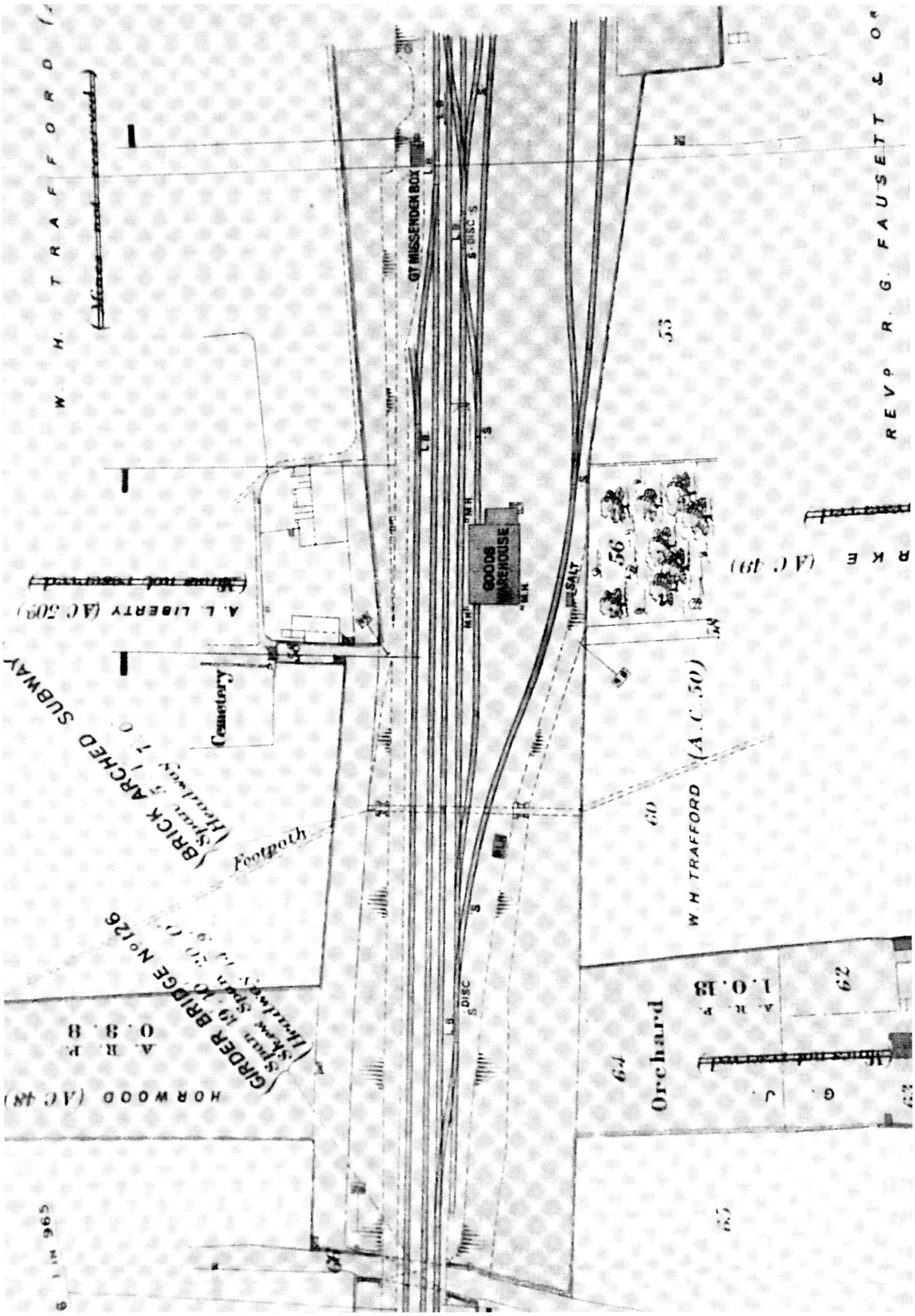

Ground plan of the goods yard at Great Missenden in 1908. The goods shed at Great Missenden was demolished on June 6, 1969.

John Mock Collection

Great Missenden Looking north in the 1930's.

H C Casserley

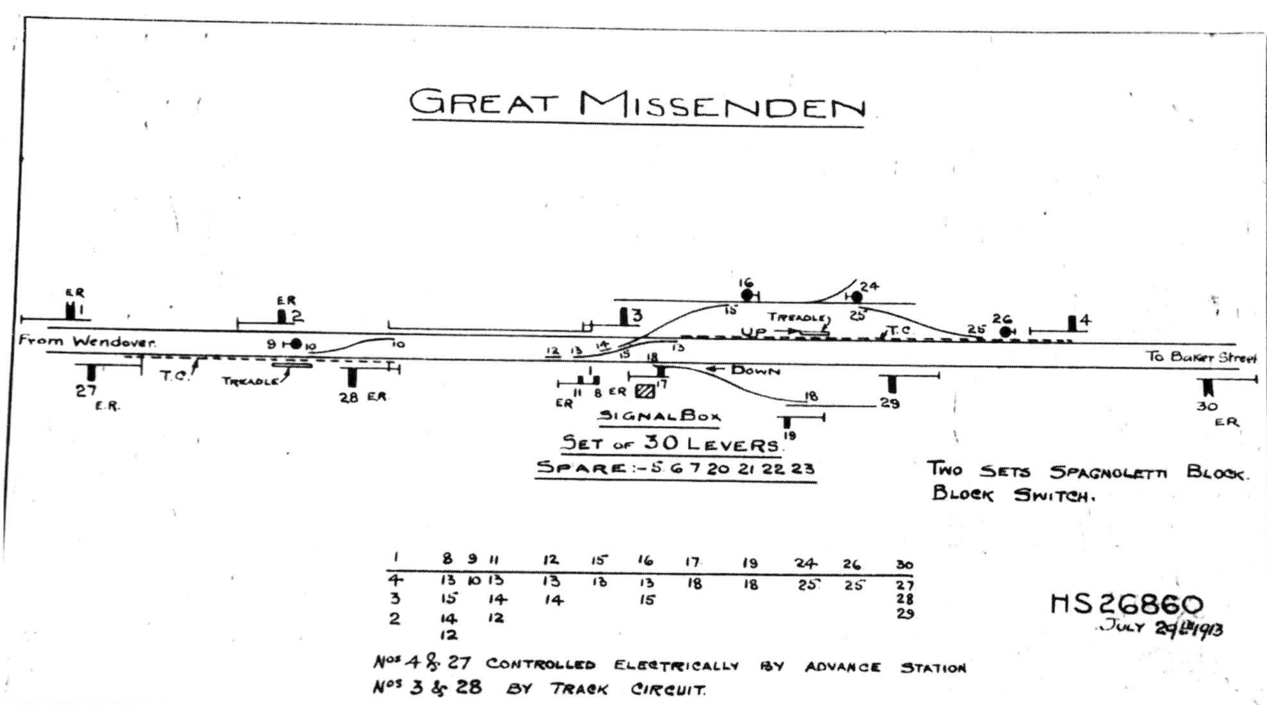

Signalling diagram from 1913.

Mike Crosbie Collection

Great Missenden virtually as complete, with Goods yard, water tower and signal box in the early 1950's.
London Underground Railway Society Collection

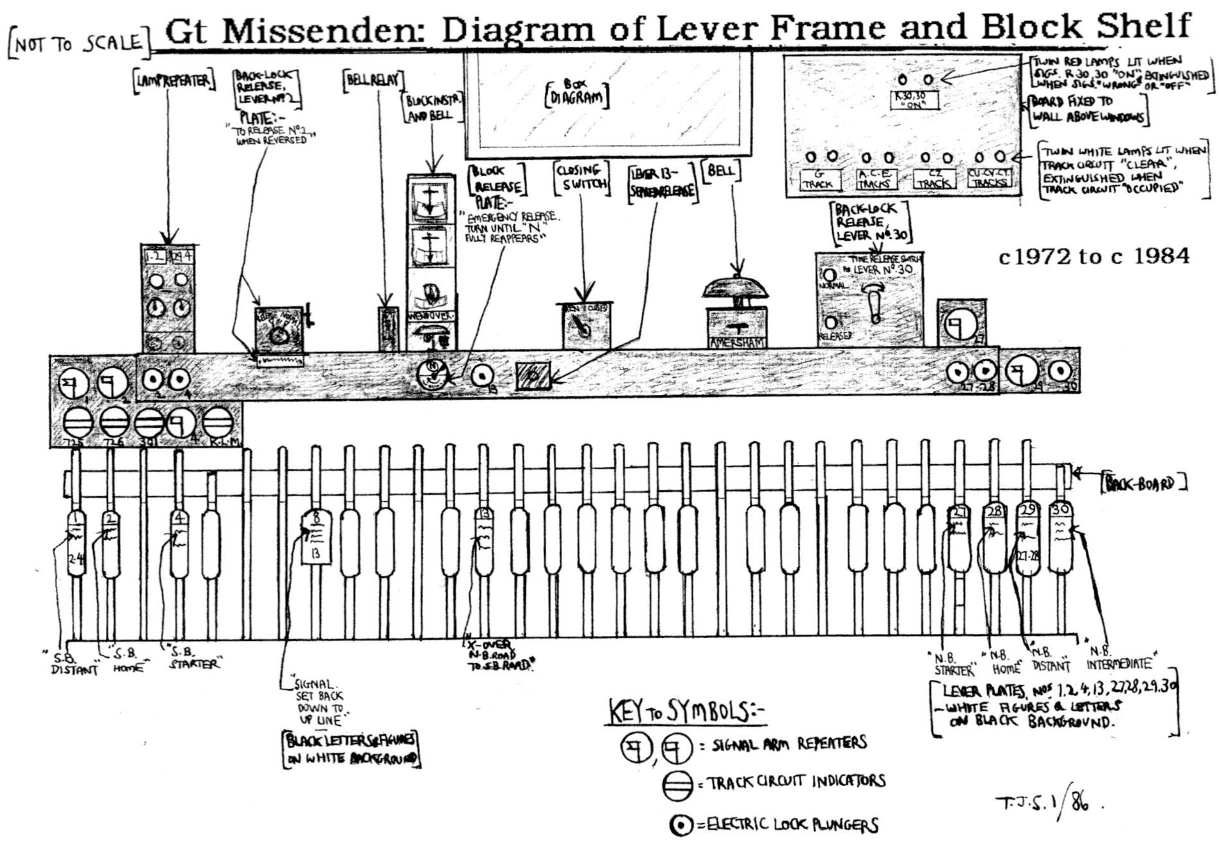

Comparative signalling diagrams, data supplied by Tim Stevens

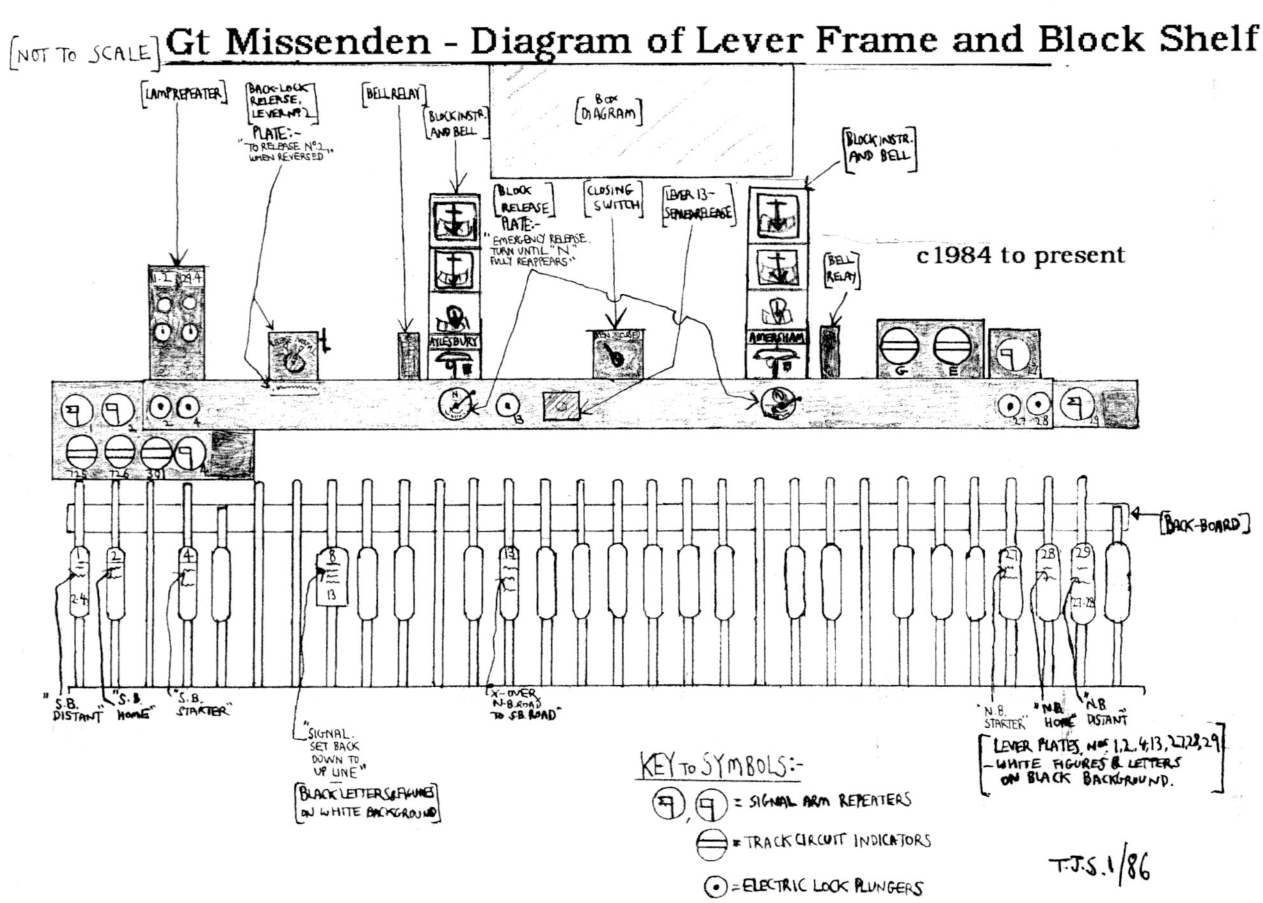

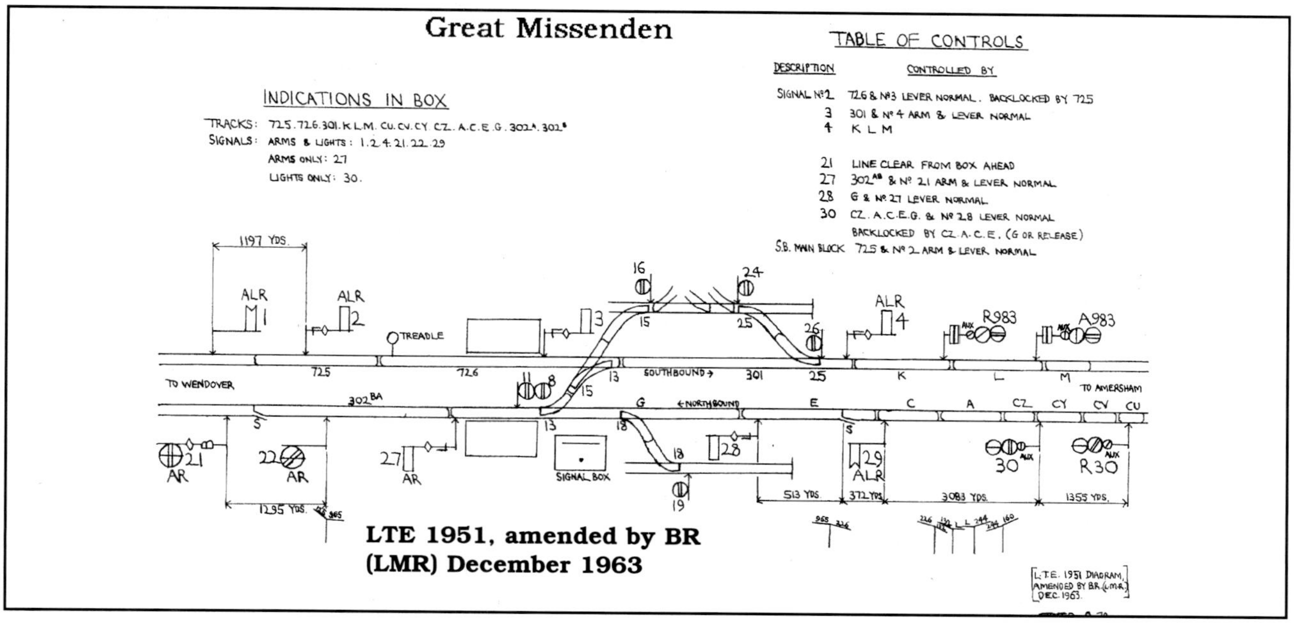

LTE 1951, amended by BR (LMR) December 1963

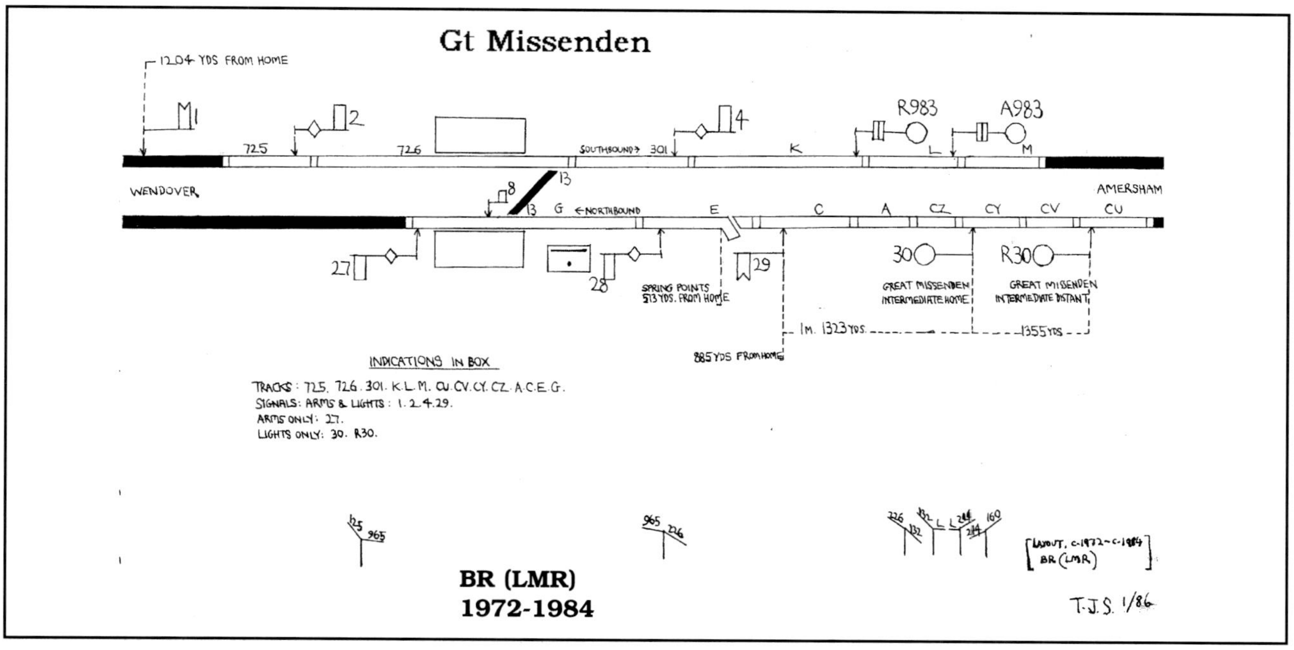

BR (LMR) 1972-1984

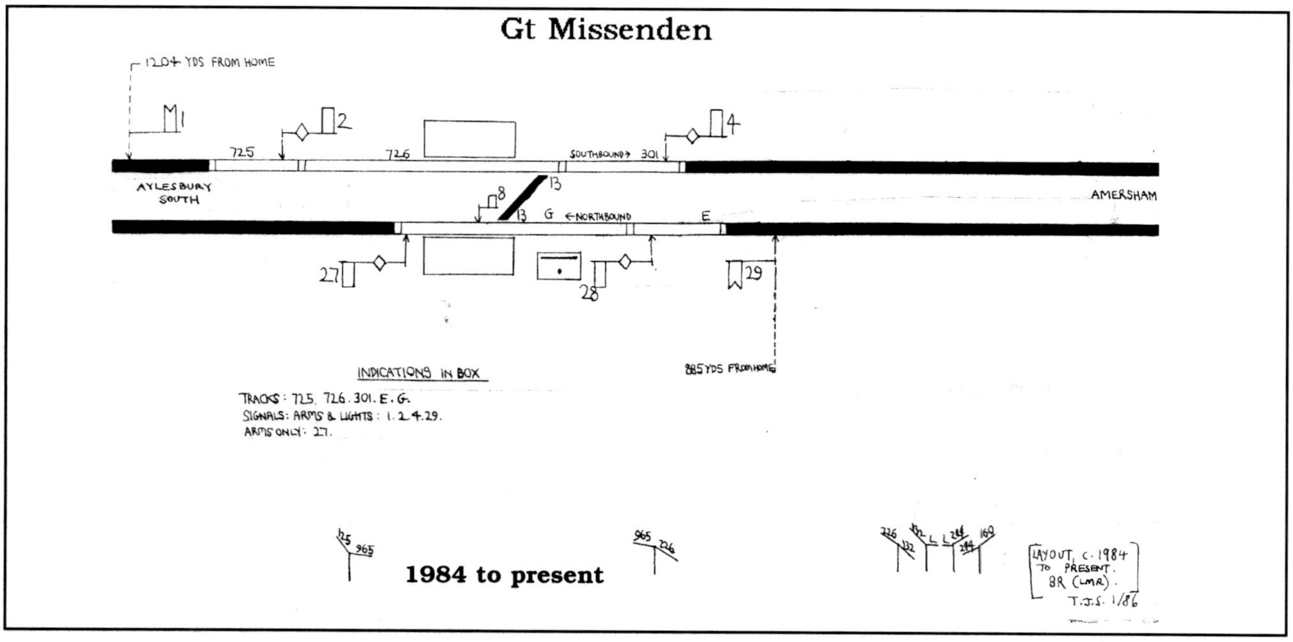

1984 to present

An A class engine no 23 on a goods train near Dutchlands summit heading for Aylesbury. The train appears to be largely composed of Stephenson Clarke coal wagons with some other private owner wagons near the brake van. As this is in the days of London Transport it would be amongst the few years in the early thirties when they still operated goods trains.

H Gordon Tidey courtesy of the National Railway Museum

B1 4-6-0 61157 shunting at Aylesbury in February 1964.

A Doyle / Colour-Rail 481

'Jubilee 4-6-0 45709 'Implacable' heads through Amersham on its way to Aylesbury with brown compartment stock in May 1963. Held on one of two reversing sidings is Electric loco no 5 'John Hampden' at the very limits of electrification.

Colour-Rail LT38

The slightly over idealised cover of the 'Metroland' guide for 1930. The guide is part of the collection of Mr T M L Wayman who has had difficulty in finding the years 1917 and 1918, or even finding out if one was produced for those years. Should any reader be aware of information on these years the publishers would be grateful to receive the information on behalf of Mr Wayman.

The Aylesbury station looking north in the early 1980's when, as can be seen, the bay platform was still in use with a train on the
right.

An oil painting by the author of an 'H' class 4-4-4 tank depicting the open land area north of Rickmansworth in the 1920's and 1930's before development and mature trees made it more enclosed.

Bill Simpson courtesy of R M Casserley

A superb watercolour painting by Brian Payne of the steam working days of the Halton Camp Railway crossing over the Wendover Arm of the Grand Union Canal. The loco is one of the 0-4-0 saddletanks.

Still life of a terminus, the open door of the T stock that forms the Chesham shuttle, with a truck piled with parcels. Chesham, a week after steam had ended, in September 1960.

Ray Oakley / Colour Rail LT276

One of 'E' class 0-4-4T L44 at Neasden in May 1961.

Colour-Rail LT21

A sunny day on the Bluebell Railway in 2003 and the gleaming Metropolitan stock of the one time Chesham branch runs as a special train behind a tender engine of the South Eastern & Chatham Railway. A scene of near perfection in railway elegance.

Bill Simpson

Chesham in September 1961, electric loco no 16 'Oliver Goldsmith' having brought in the 13.34 from Liverpool Street is in the process of running round its train of Dreadnought stock at Chesham. The stock will then return as empty stock to Neasden, an A60 set waits in the bay. All the old rolling stock on Watford, Chesham and Amersham services were replaced in 1961/62 with new aluminium 'A' (Amersham) stock.

G Hunt/Colour-Rail LT194

Stoke Mandeville in 2003, painting and refurbishment of the stations north of Rickmansworth by Chiltern Railways deserves a great deal of credit to all concerned. The stations are splendidly restored and although railways are always the convenient butt of discontent, this railway could not be more finely and efficiently presented.

Bill Simpson

A C13 no 67418 on the Chesham shuttle with the Ashbury stock in 1955.

Colour-Rail BRE1344

A train from Aylesbury calling at Wendover in the summer of 2003. The new by-pass added in the 1990's was an obvious benefit to the town, but detracted a great deal from the 'country' feel of the station area.

An enduring memory for passing trains, the sculpture of Mr Bernard Carter in the garden at Stoke Mandeville station.
Bill Simpson

One of the K class 114 at Amersham in 1938

Colour-Rail LT2

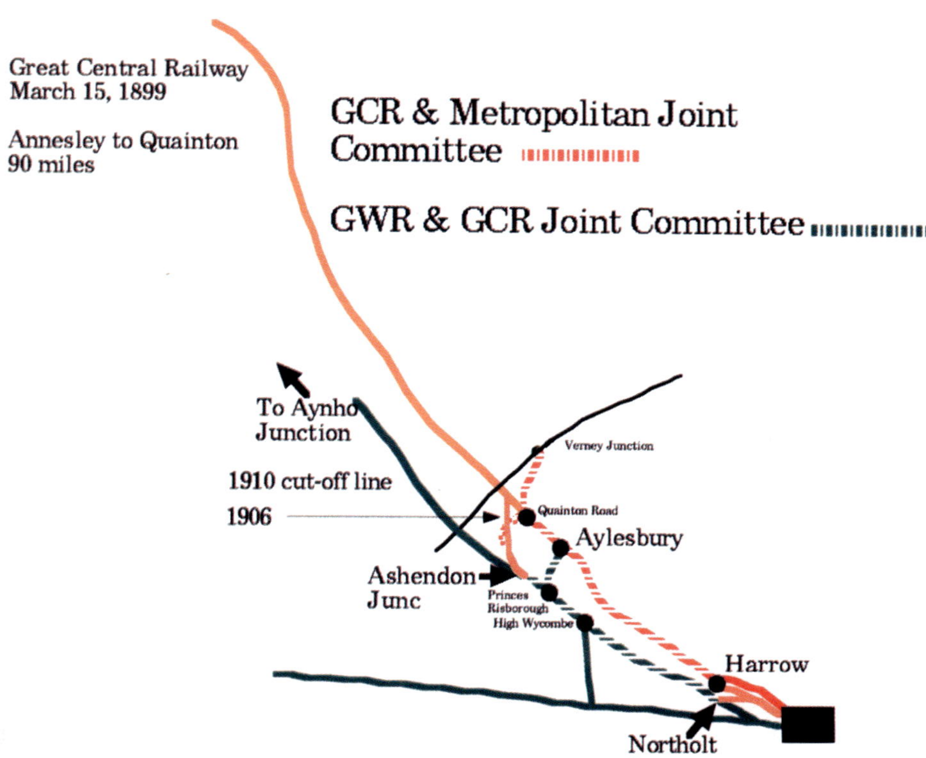

A simplified diagrammatic view of the arrangement of lines in relationship with the Great Central Railway. From Harrow the lines went to their respective London termini. The short section to the west of Quainton Road, passing under the GCR connecting line, is the Wotton Tramway, later Oxford & Aylesbury Tramway.

Wendover station looking north in the 1930's.

H C Casserley

Chapter Eight
Wendover

At thirty three and a half miles from Baker Street the Metropolitan guide called Wendover the 'pearl' of the Chilterns. That is understandable, it is a very pleasant tree enclosed town with many fine old buildings. The railway cut through the rising ground from the cross roads and church at the lower eastern end. It also cut through a footpath. This was carried alongside the platform over the connection bridge to the field beyond. To relieve the town a by pass was constructed in the 1990's and this runs immediately alongside the railway.

Close by Wendover is the grandly ornate Halton House, once the home of Alfred de Rothschild. He regularly used the LNWR station at Tring to reach London but with the opening of the Metropolitan at Wendover he chose to travel from there using a first class compartment. To cater more appropriately for the new VIP the Met purchased two 32 ft long six-wheeled saloons from Brown Marshalls at £660 each. These provided all amenities including a servants compartment.

The saloons were also used by the Met board, in particular with the opening of the Uxbridge branch.

With the arrival of GCR and their section from Harrow to Marylebone he was of the

Wendover 'down' platform early in the twentieth century.

Peter Nicholls Collection

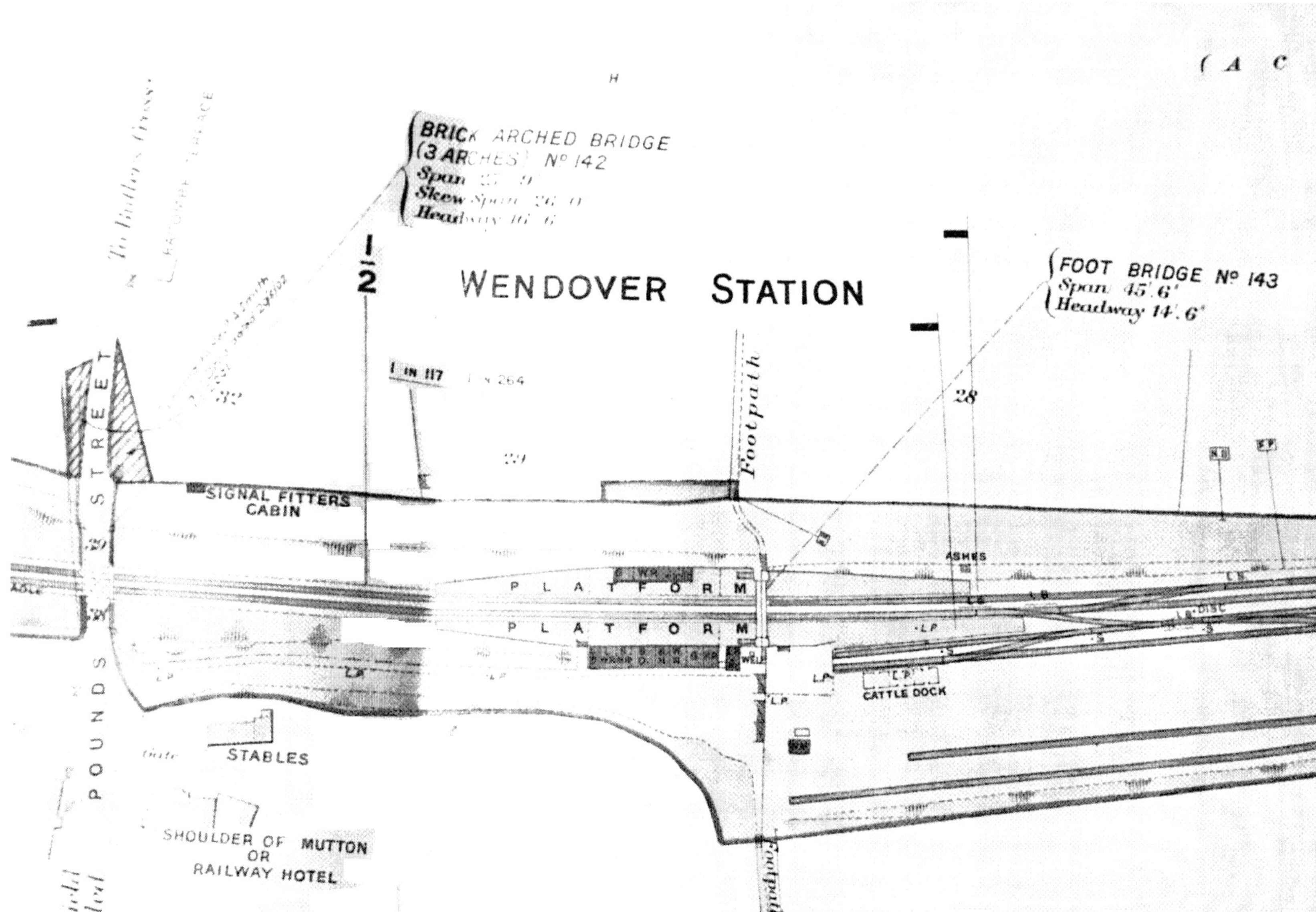

Wendover ground plan of station in 1908. Note the unusual situation that had to be accommodated by the railway of continuing the public footpath across the station separate from the platforms crossover bridge. This had to be continued recently with the building of the new by-pass when it was extended above the roadway. A feature of Wendover also was the way that the 'up' platform fitted to the bay which was utilised by the Halton Camp Railway using this bay as a terminus

John Mock Collection

Fairburn tank no 42231 of Neasden shed in Wendover station on July 26, 1958 with an Aylesbury Baker Street train.
H C Casserley

persuasion to arrive at the new terminus of Marylebone. To retain his patronage, which was worth £600 per annum, the Met decided to splice the two saloons into one long 36ft vehicle at a cost of £220 and brought it into service early in 1907. The new vehicle was modified to include a kitchenette with stove, sink and sideboard eventually becoming 55ft 10in long.

Predictably to follow the new advantages of travel he was inclined to avail himself of the motor car. An advantage possibly, but unlikely to reach the same level of luxury.

The vehicle remained a VIP saloon used on the opening of the Watford and Stanmore branches. In the prospect of closure of the line it made one remarkable visit to Brill. How the comparison must have looked, with this fine coach alongside the rickety platform at Brill terminus would have made a fine interpretation to the artist's eye. It was stored at Neasden until scrapping by the LT in the mid thirties.

There has been three coal merchants at Wendover station yard, a Mr Payne, Mr Rance and Mr Caudrey all had private owner wagons delivering to the yard.

Wendover in 1983, now drastically changed. All the structures on the left have been removed, including one interesting building with steps leading up to it. Possibly an old lamp room? Also removed are the trees on the right where the new by-pass road now exists. Modern trains are now the Chiltern Railway's Turbos.
Bill Simpson

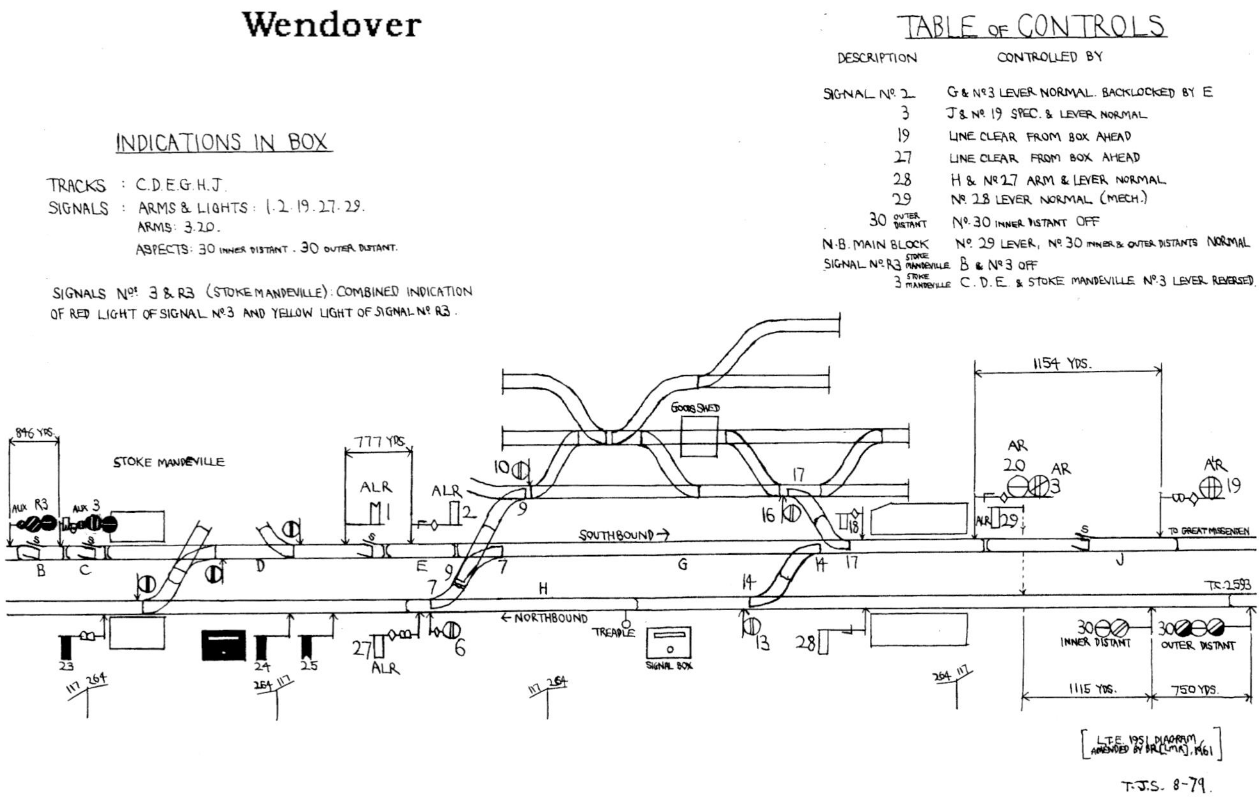

Details of signalling at Wendover kindly supplied by Tim Stevens. Note siding between goods shed and main running lines which was for a time part of the Halton Camp Railway

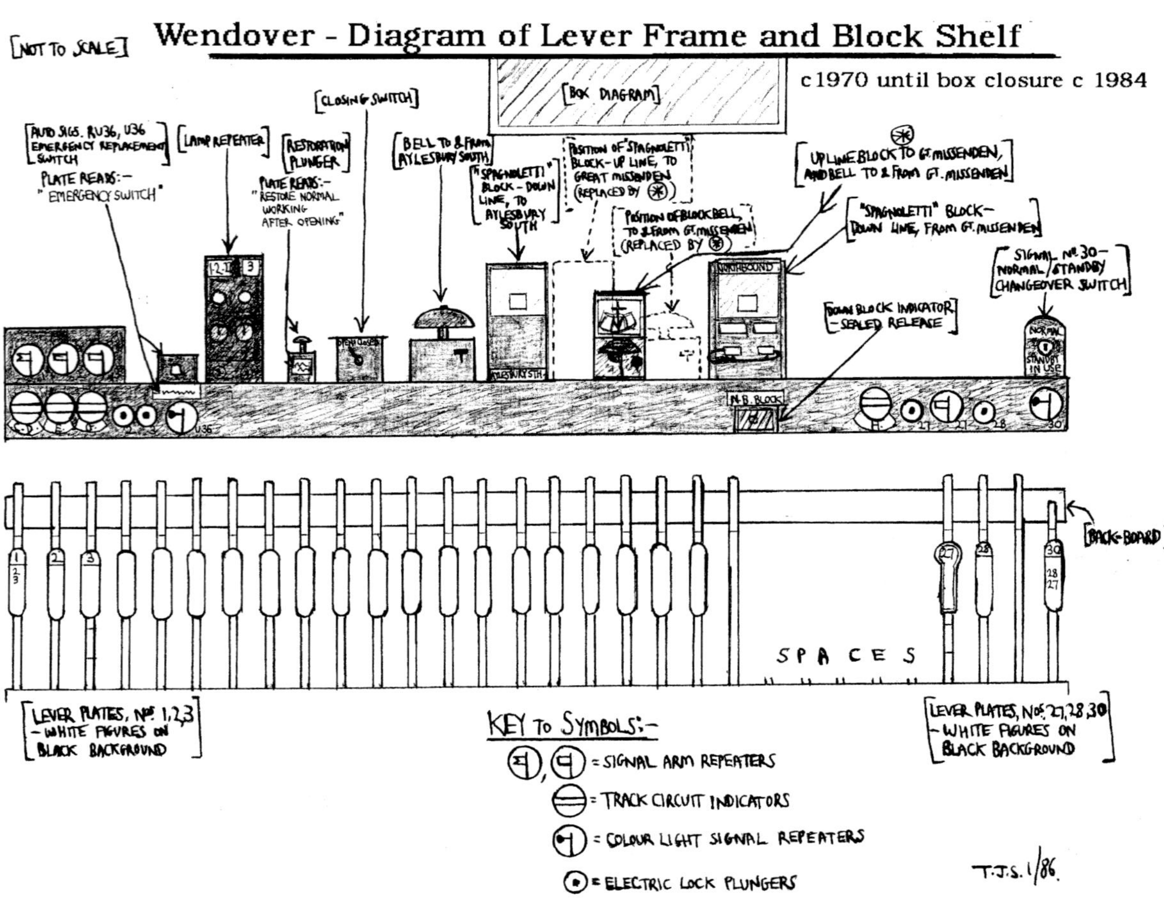

Wendover signal box in 1985, shortly before it was demolished.

Bill Simpson

Wendover

Layout c1970 to c1984 box closure

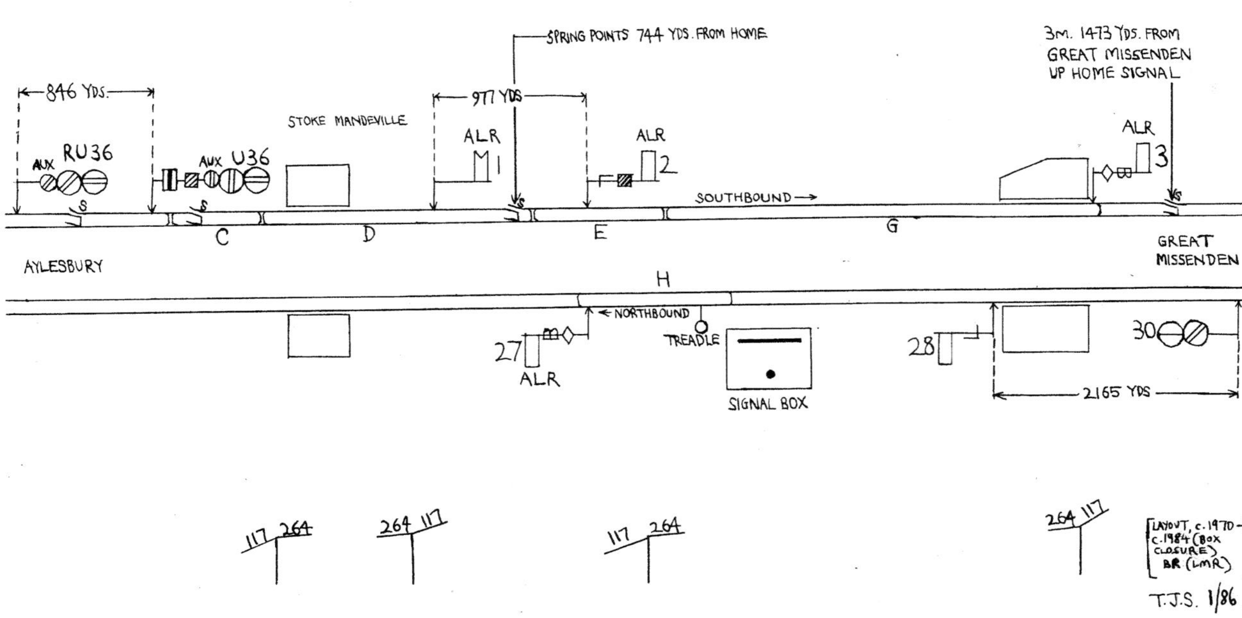

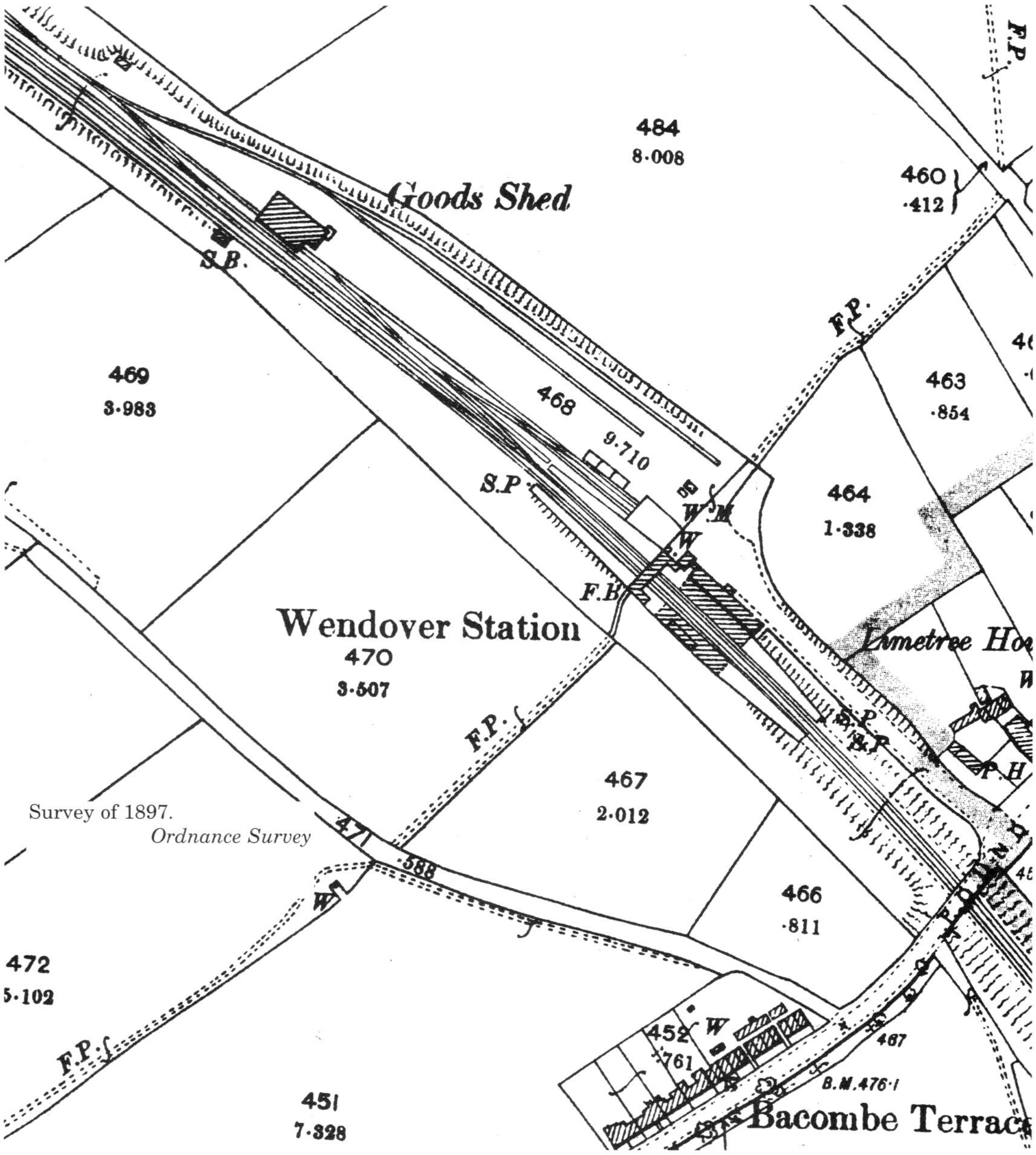

Survey of 1897.

Ordnance Survey

Not ideally clear, the station at about the time of the map above, but it is possible to make out the well stocked goods yard on the left and cattle dock. Between there and the station is the bridge over the platforms that also to carried the footpath into the foreground field.

Peter Nicholls Collection

Diesel hauled train AMW 188 near the bridge over canal on the Halton Railway

A J Reed

Halton Camp Railway

The house of Halton near Wendover was the home of Mr Alfred de Rothschild who was requested to take out an occupation of his lands early in the First World War for the military. He agreed and the new volunteer army of 1914 was encamped there. This was a temporary expedient until accommodation could be built for the soldiers in the form of huts.

This camp, built by Sir Robert McAlpine, became a Royal Flying Corps Training Camp in 1916. It was a maintenance facility with some 10,000 personnel under training. The Royal Air Force section of the services continued to use it as a training camp and still does.

At Wendover, adjoining the station, was the railway branch line that served the camp. This curved away from the station to the east of the main line. It was standard gauge and of $1^3/_4$ miles in length. The survey to construct the line must have been the most rudimentary imaginable, as Mr Thomas William Reade, Stationmaster of Wendover station in 1915, did, as directed by the company, take a Sunday morning stroll with his son from the north end of Wendover station to Halton. Along the way he surveyed a route for a simple line of railway to be constructed which he presented to the Metropolitan Railway board at Baker Street. This was not only approved by them but they also appropriated £350 for him to purchase a house in Chiltern Road, Wendover. A very advantageous Sunday morning walk, one would conclude.

With military approval, the railway was built by German pow's who were held at Halton. It was opened for use in 1917. To assist the construction, a narrow gauge railway was also built, this carried supplies using a Kerr Stewart 0-4-0ST. The standard gauge railway ran from a specially constructed platform on the 'up' side of Wendover station and terminated close to the workshops near Chestnut Avenue.

Probably, with much regret, Alfred de Rothschild gave permission for beech trees to be felled from the woodland on the estate above Tring Road, so serious was the demand for timber. As an aid to this the railway of standard gauge was provided with a feeder railway in the form of an extension to the existing narrow gauge railway which was extended to access the woodland and supply the railhead of its larger associate. Both railways operated with steam power and it must have provided a scene of great interest as the timber was removed from tipper trucks to wagons for the standard gauge to take to the station. The timber was intended for trench supports on the western front. The narrow gauge system seems to have disappeared early in World War Two.

Although the line was intended wholly as an industrial undertaking it seems to have taken on an impromptu role for airmen travelling to the station, hitching a ride in its trucks

After the war the intensive use of the little line was reduced, but it still continued with the hardly demanding job of carrying coal supplies to feed the camp boilers.

There was no passenger service to Halton Camp as the light railway from the Met station was officially a goods only line, needless to say this was not strictly adhered to. At Aylesbury, Queens Park Coaches ran a competitive service from Aylesbury on a route via Kingsbury, Weston Turville and the Camp. This is one of their Dennis coaches on the square at Aylesbury in 1951. Queens Park Coaches were taken over by Eastern National.

Mr Albin J Reed

Entrance weighbridge and attendant hut at Upper Icknield Way, Halton.

Albin J Reed

Saddletank 0-6-0 'Southport'.

Peter Nicholls Collection

After the war the camp became a training ground for the newly formed air corps that became the Royal Air Force. Thus was the line happily occupied in its coal carrying work until the boilers were converted to oil firing in the late 1950's, much of the country was being affected by the Clean Air Act of that time reducing combustion of solid fuel. The oil fuel was delivered directly by road tanker. This left the railway with even less to do and the state of the hurridly constructed permanent way was beginning to show serious wear.

Consequently the last train left Halton ceremoniously on March 29, 1963 and the line officially closed on March 31.

First locomotive used on the line is unclear, it is doubtful that the Metropolitan would have any locomotives that could operate the system, even if they had been available. The greater likelihood would be small tank engines displaced from railway engineering work, as those that had worked on the London Extension of the MS&LR, when on completion left hundreds of such engines that were sold off by contractors.

An Hawthorn Leslie 0-4-0ST called 'Benton' arrived in 1917 but this struggled with the 1 in 39 gradient between the Aylesbury Road and Dobbins Lane Crossing. This engine, probably exhausted, was withdrawn in 1918.

In 1919 a Hunslet 0-6-0ST called 'Southport' was supplied, also a Manning Wardle class 'M' 0-6-0 side tank named 'Birkenhead' no 112 on arrival, renamed 'Halton'. Both engines had been acquired surplus from the Ministry of Munitions, Gretna.

Another 0-6-0 Manning Wardle arrived, with an Air Ministry number of 103, whilst another Hawthorn Leslie engine of the 0-4-0 type came once more in 1925 to see if it would be suitable for the branch. It had an axle load of $13^1/_2$ tons and was regarded as unsuitable, which gives a good indication of the sustainable quality of the permanent way.

It seems that steam was supplanted on this line before the main lines, as diesel mechanicals, from John Fowler & Co of Leeds, began to put in an appearance in the early forties. An 0-6-0 Air Ministry no 188 was delivered new in 1940 followed by an 0-4-0 type no 219 in 1941. Steam locomotives were probably reduced to storage with their arrival. Continuing the modern traction two more 0-4-0's were delivered, no 223 from Air Ministry, Heywood and no 240 from Air Ministry, Henlow, which arrived in

Even in full use it would have been the most basic of a railway terminus. The platform and large goods store at the end of the railway. Where the car is would have been where the track was at one time.

Bill Simpson Courtesy of RAF Halton

1955. No 223 was given the duty of hauling the last train, with due ceremony.

The narrow gauge locomotive was a Kerr Stuart 'Wren' class of 60 cms gauge no 1252 it came from the Fovent Military Railway and was used for logging duties. It was sold at auction together with much of the narrow gauge track at the camp in August 1922.

Various wagons carried lettering of the post grouping companies LMS and LNER and some BR.

The Line

Much information was compiled by the late Tony Coldwell in this account of the line. He, in all honesty, admitted that where precise knowledge was not available he used enlightened guesswork.

'The platform at Wendover station was probably built of railway sleepers and covered in two inch thick planking as an extension to the brick built main station platform on the 'up' side. In later years it was partially separated by a fence.

A two road shunt was installed by the Metropolitan railway adjacent to the north end of the 'up' main line platform in 1892. As these were adjoining the coal staithes they would be mainly for that purpose.

The Halton branch was protected by a GCR signal from the west of the three yard sidings. Some time after the First World War the goods sidings accommodation was enlarged with the addition of a bay platform adjoining a cattle dock. Proceeding beyond the area between the main line and the goods shed there were a set of gates. (These almost certainly marked the boundry between the Met & GCR Joint and Military. Engines of the former, in the normal circumstances of the main line railway would be restricted from passing beyond these.) These gates lead to a section with double track, a loop, this converged again to single just south of the first foot/field crossing. The line then commenced along a gentle curve embankment. Along past the rear gardens of houses towards Dobbins Lane and another foot/field crossing. It continued through what are now the rear gardens of Lionel Avenue, these houses continuing up to Aylesbury Road level crossing. Just before this crossing a long passing loop was installed on the west of the line which could accommodate about twelve vehicles. Initially trains were hauled in both directions on this loop which was also used as a run-round for locomotives when propelling a train into Wendover station yard. The only run-round in Wendover yard was on the lines used by the goods shed which would

Saddletank 0-6-0 no 103

Peter Nicholls Collection

be regularly in use, sometimes with vehicles stored on them. Some of them being wagons to be collected for the camp. In later years trains were hauled to Halton and 'pushed' back to Wendover to avoid this run-round operation. Either way things would require some observant and effective brake control. From the crossing the line took a direct course running alongside the recreation ground. Just north of this play area is another foot/field crossing. Sixty yards north of this crossing is a fine brick culvert that carried the railway over a stream. Three hundred yards north of this, the line reaches the Wendover arm of the Grand Junction (Union) Canal. The first bridge was constructed of railway sleepers whilst an order was made with the Cleveland Bridge Company for a more permanent structure. This was installed and went into use until 1965 when the Royal Engineers removed it. The canal had always suffered from serious leakage and fell out of use as it was a problem for the main canal'. At present the Wendover Arm Trust are working on restoration of the canal, this time without the leaks.

'The line continues on a slight embankment crossing fields and passing through woodland until it reaches the camp system.

About 500 yards short of the terminus was sited a short headshunt which was west of the line to Halton, near here was an east spur leading to the Tring Road. This spur forked into five sidings on different levels, the highest being alongside Frank Woods Yard who was a contractor to the RAF for building work and supplies. The middle level, with two or three sidings, was at one time used as a run-round. The lowest siding provided engine servicing facilities.

At the terminus, trains entering the station went beneath a sheerlegs gantry that was used for any heavy loading of equipment. The line then passes the engineering building before arriving alongside the canopied large goods stores building. The last building was the Stationmaster's office and small goods stores. The terminus had a passing loop for run-round which had a set of points to access the bakery building platform and the boiler house where coal wagons were shunted. Coal was shovelled from the wagons by hand onto a chute that took it under the boiler house.

The boiler house powered the generators to produce electricity for the camp using Belliss & Morcombe 'A' open frame engines and generators. These were later dismantled to install a more modified system.'

Very little is viewable today, the station yard at Wendover has become a car park and Business Park, but with free pedestrian access to reach a continuing footpath at the other end. This footpath is on the trackbed of the Halton Camp line. As Tony described it, it is carried on

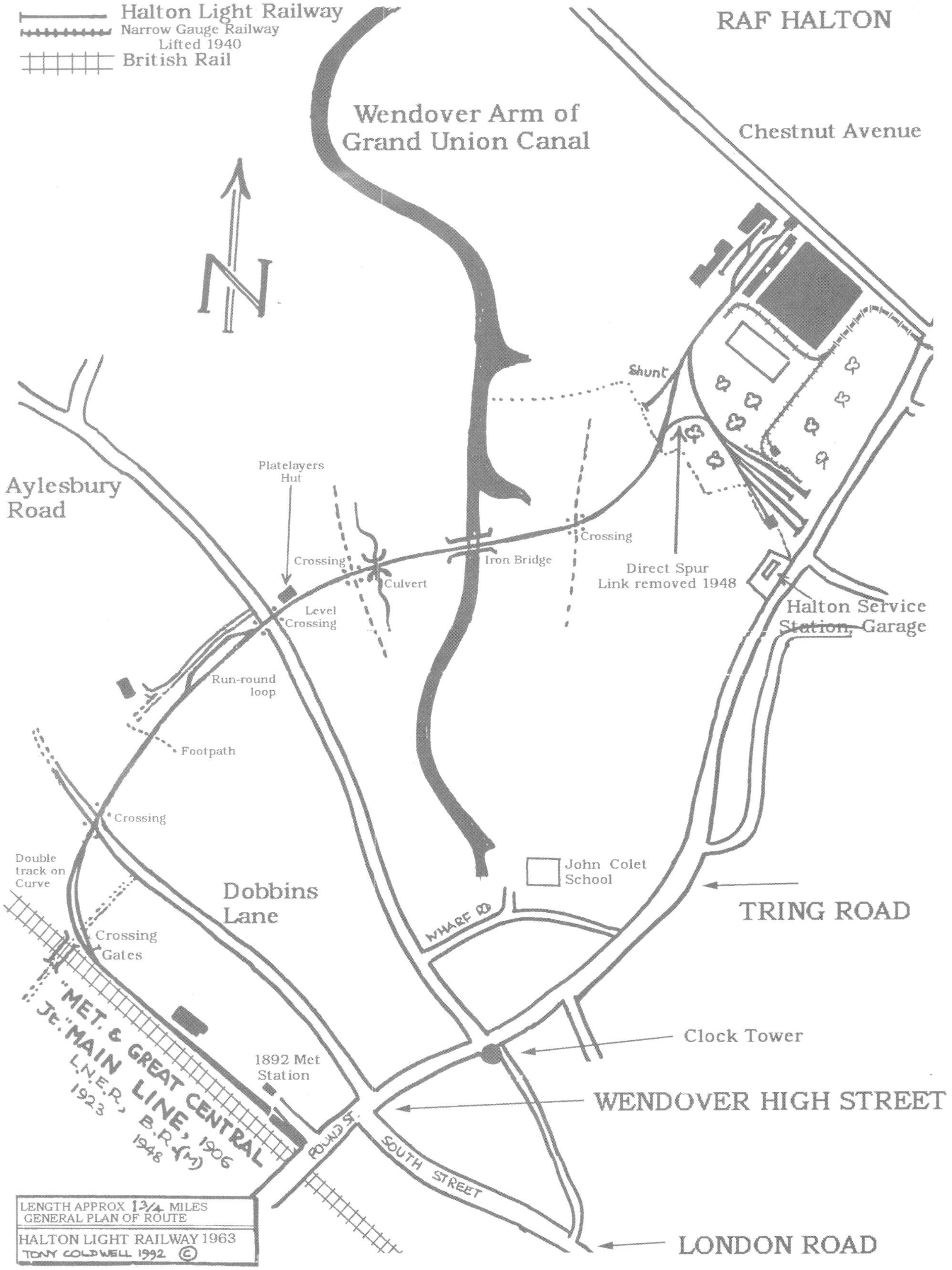

The Halton Camp Railway branch from the station at Wendover.

Tony Coldwell

The level crossing for the Halton Camp Railway on the Aylesbury Road.

C Blunden

a higher elevation along the backs of houses and onto a new development. The path still continues on, alongside the recreation field and rises quite markedly. The canal now has a special footbridge to cross it that has replaced the former railway bridge. And in the reveries of a walk on a pleasant day, it is easy to imagine the stubby little tank engine clanking across with its selection of various railway initials lettered on its trucks and gathering its strength for the rising ground that follows. This ground is pleasantly canopied under overhanging trees. Quite abruptly the evidence of once-a-railway ends at a field gate stile. There is nothing whatsoever to see on the distance from there to the camp, for this has long since been turned over by the plough.

A lorry of the Met - LNER Joint in the yard at Wendover.

Peter Nicholls Collection

Some irony for German pow's gathering timber for trench supports on the narrow gauge trucks, it is to be hoped that there are no very tight curves for the log over two vehicles in the foreground!

Peter Nicholls Collection

Troops leaving the train at Wendover station during the army period.

Peter Nicholls Collection

The 0-4-0 narrow gauge locomotove 'Wren', it is considered that the surviving 0-4-0 on the Leighton Buzzard Narrow Gauge Railway 'Pixie' is a very fair comparison.

Tony Coldwell Collection

The narrow gauge in practice, which involves locomotives working with personnel in handling vehicles; in this case pow's.

Peter Nicholls Collection

Loco AMW 188 waiting to cross A413 Aylesbury Road with a train for Halton on April 5, 1948.
A J Reed

Railway crossing gates on A413 Aylesbury Road east side on June 7, 1965, replaced 1997 when eighty years old.
A J Reed

One of the steam locomotives Black Hawthorn locomotive 'Benton' at Stablesbridge Curve at the north end of Wendover yard.
Tony Coldwell

A Manning Wardle class 'M' originally called 'Birkenhead' to be renamed 'Halton' no 112 at the camp. Here it is seen being examined by its crew just north of the Aylesbury Road level crossing in 1936.
J H Venn

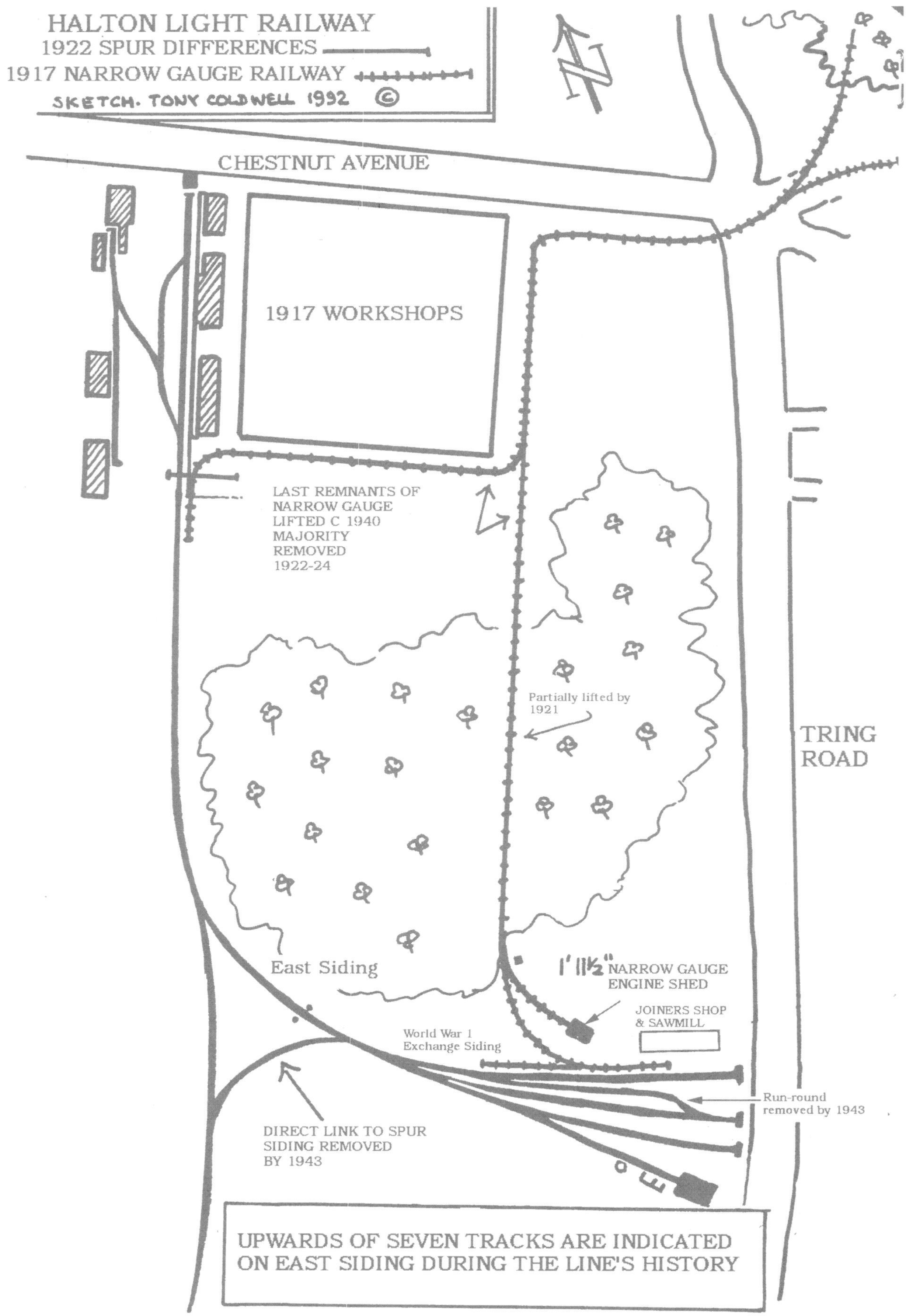

Enlarged section of workshop area in 1917.

Tony Coldwell

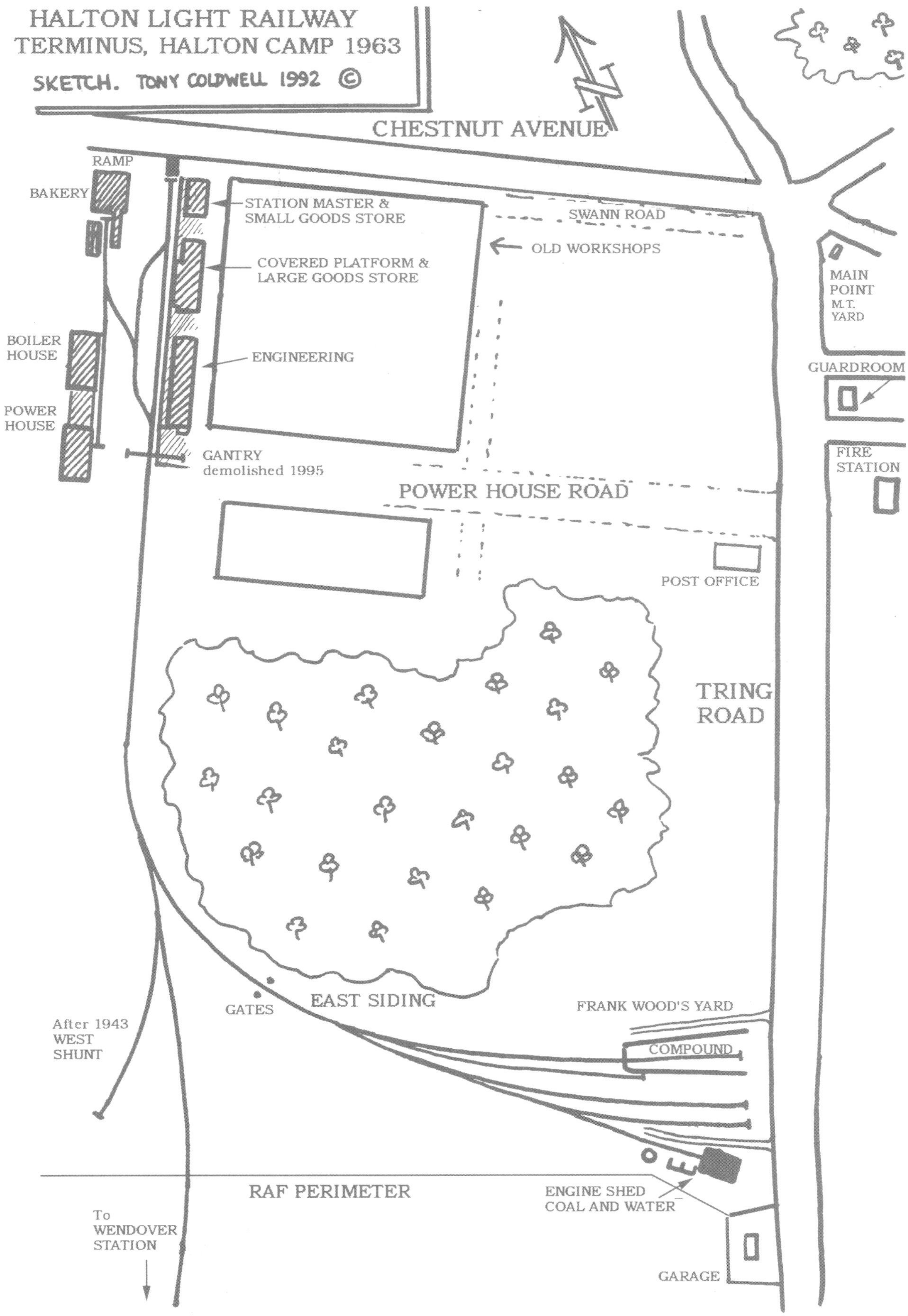

Enlarged section of workshop area in 1963.

Tony Coldwell

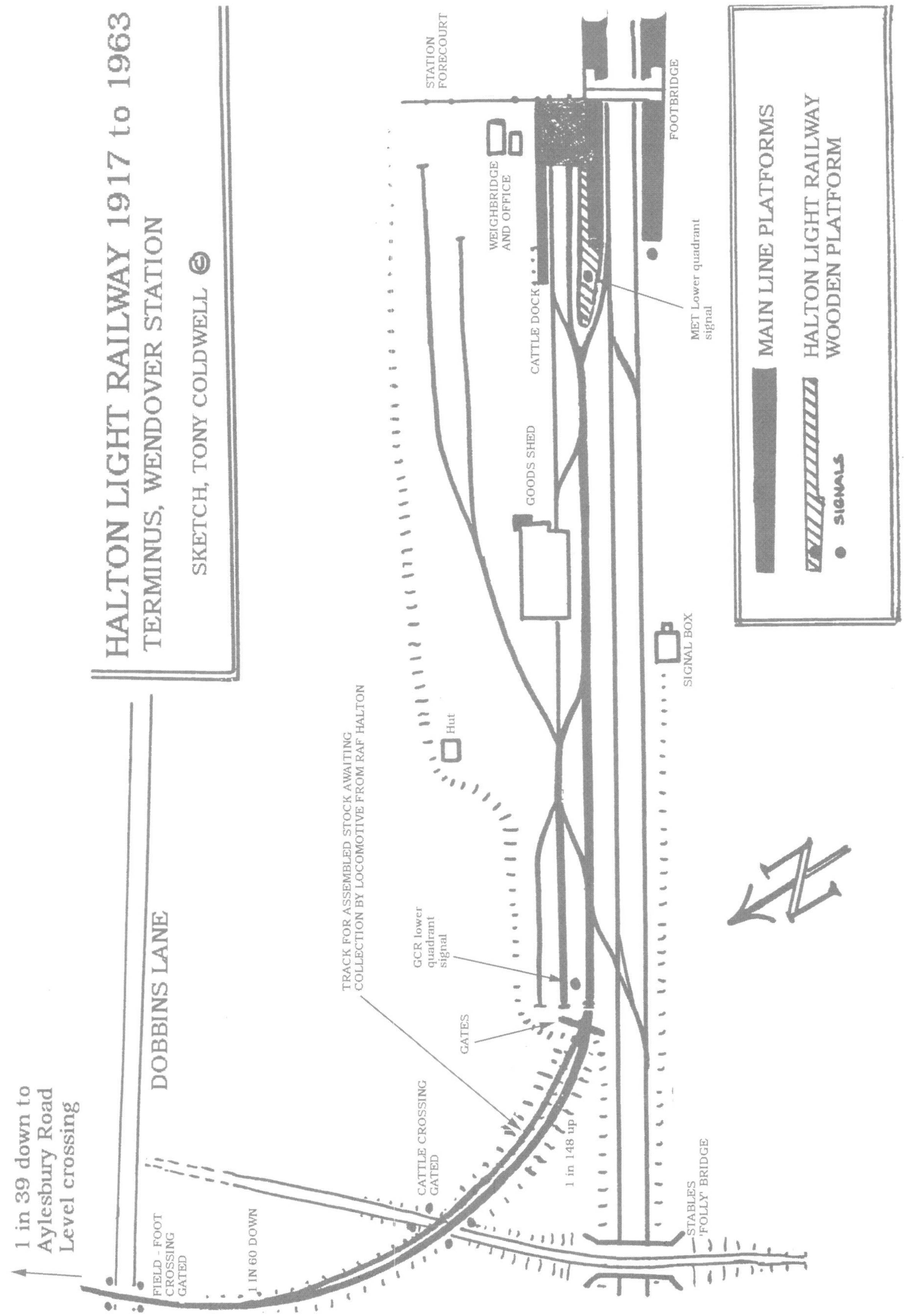

Tony Coldwell

Integration of the railway to the goods yard at Wendover

Loco AMW 219 approaching bridge on west side with train for Halton on August 21, 1952.

A J Reed

Points at beginning of the loop for wagon storage, immediately on the camp side of the boundary gates, this view leading to Wendover station, on August 4, 1959.

A J Reed

Remarkable view looking from the Halton Camp line into the goods yard with GCR signal protecting entrance to the yard. All of this is completely built over now.

A J Reed

Even the modest but formerly essential Halton Camp Railway was entitled to its grand finale which took place in March 1963
Bucks Herald

The north end of the wagon storage loop (right hand track) just outside gates at entrance to Wendover yard. In the distance, post for Dobbins Lane foot crossing and gradient post. In the foreground John Reed and companion.
John Reed

Probably one of the last views taken north of the station in 1985, before everything changed. The Goods shed and signalbox were demolished shortly afterwards and a few years later the new road by-pass was built where the pylons stand. The goods bay on the right was used by Halton Camp trains.

BIll Simpson

Locomotives of the Halton Light Railway on the standard gauge of 4ft 8½in

Number or name		Whel.armnt	Cyls	Mkrs	Mkrs no	Blt	Ref	Ref
	BENTON	0-4-0ST	OC	BH	1099	1896	(a)	(1)
	INCE	0-4-0ST	OC	HE	425	1887		
			reb	HE		1901	(b)	(3)
	SOUTHPORT	0-6-0ST	IC	HE	392	1886	(c)	(5)
No 112	HALTON	0-6-0T	IC	MW	1100	1888	(d)	s/s after 6/1938
	-	0-4-0ST	OC	WB	*		(e)	(2)
	-	0-4-0ST	OC	HL			(f)	(4)
AMWB 103		0-6-0ST	IC	MW	212	1866		
				reb	HC	1907	(g)	(8)
AMW No 188		0-6-0DM		JF	22885	1940	New	(9)
AMW No 219		0-4-0DM		JF	22966	1941	New	(6)
AMW No 223		0-4-0DM		JF	22970	1942	(h)	(7)
AMW No 240		0-4-0DM		JF	22994	1942	(i)	(7)

* 'Surplus' 1/4/1922 and 'Machinery Market' 14/4/1922 stated that Hubert & Flint were to auction on 3-5/5/1922, re RAF Halton, plant including two locos by MW and WB; the WB loco has not yet been identified. However 'Engineer' 2/1/1920 and 'Machinery Market' 9/1/1920 stated that Hubert & Flint were to auction on 2/1/1920 re Ministry of Munitions No 1 Anti Gas Factory, Watford, plant including WB locosNOGI, four-wheel coupled 10 x 15in cyls. This was WB 1493/1896 and since MW 212 came here from Watford, it is possible that WB 1493 came here also.

(a) Ex H M Nowell, East India Dock Improvements (1912-c1950) contract London

(b) Earlier G Trollope & Sons and Colis & Sons Ltd, Oldham Aircraft Factory contract, Lancs. until 7/1919 at least; here by 4/1920.

(c) Ex Ministry of Munitions, Gretna, Dumfriesshire, SOUTHPORT, after 15/12/1920 by 4/1921. (Advertised for sale at Gretna in 'Surplus' of 15/11/1920. Possibly to Air Ministry, Watford, Herts (for repairs?), by 2/1924; returned after 3/1924 by 9/1932.

(d) Arrived here after 17/7/1911 by 11/1929; earlier Logan & Hemingway, contractors. Possibly ex Ministry of Munitions, Gretna, /1920 (a MW 0-6-0 tank), 13 in cylinders. 'No 4 DES 123' was advertised for sale at Ministry of Munitions, Gretna, Dumfriesshire, in 'Surplus' of 15/11/1920; (this loco may be HALTON).

(e) Origin and identity uncertain, but see ref*

(f) Ex HL, loan /1925

(g) Ex Air Ministry, Watford, Herts

(h) Ex JF, Leeds, after rebuilding, 10/1954; earlier Air Ministry, Heywood, Lancs.

(i) Ex JF, Leeds after rebuilding, 3/1955; earlier Air Ministry Henlow, Beds.

(1) Later Ministry of Munitions, Woolston Rolling Mills, Southampton, Hampshire, by 6/1919; for sale there 4/1923.

(2) For sale 5/5/1922; s/s

(3) Here until 11/1920 at least; spares ordered by RAF Stores Dept. Watford, Herts 8/1921 (loco may have still been there, or possibly at Watford).

(4) Returned to HL off loan/1925 (too heavy for the track)

(5) s/s after 9/1932, by 6/1938

(6) to Air Ministry, Harlow, Beds, 1/1955

(7) later Ministry of Public Buildings and Works, Burtonwood, Lancs, 4/1963

(8) to Thos W Ward Ltd, Columbia Wharf, Grays, Essex by 23/6/1949; scrapped c/1949

The Narrow gauge Railway of 2ft 0in

-	0-4-0ST	OC	KS	1252	1914	(a)	(1)
-	4wDM		RH	191661	1938	(b)	(2)

(a) New to MacDonald, Gibbs & Co. WD Fovent Camp construction contract, Wilts; Halton by 8/1922.

(b) Earlier Ministry of War Transport, Poppylot Farm, Southery, Norfolk; Halton after 20/7/1943 by 26/7/1944, possibly for storage only, although it was repaired at Halton in 1944. Spares were ordered on 26/7/1944 for 'Divisional Road Engineer, Ministry of War Transport, Bedford' for delivery to 'MWT, Halton Camp, Bucks', so the loco appears to have remained the property of the MWT.

(1) Advertised for sale at Halton Park Camp in 'Surplus' 1/8/1922, 1/9/1922-1/3/1923, 1/6/1923.If unsold then to Cohen & Armstrong Disposal Corporation, no further trace.

(2) To George W Bungay Ltd, dealers, Hayes, Middlesex, c/1950 (by 31/10/1950); resold to Dinorwic Slate Quarries Co Ltd, Llanberis, Caerns, 16/11/1950.

9) to Thos W Ward Ltd, Columbia Wharf, Grays, Essex, c/1956 (after 5/1955, by 17/10/1960); resold to Eagre Construction Co Ltd, Scunthorpe, Lincs, by 7/2/1961.

Former Metropolitan ballast brake van in the bay platform at Wendover. This bay was used by trains working to and from Halton camp.

Peter Nicholls Collection

Stoke Mandeville station looking north on July 26, 1958, The building on the right seems to have had a number of different uses. On the station plans of the Met & GCR Joint for 1909 it was used as lavatories and lamp room, it has two doorway entrances on the station side.

R M Casserley

Chapter Nine

Stoke Mandeville

Stoke Mandeville to Aylesbury is only two miles which places the former very much in the latter's shadow. It is possible for this reason that goods facilities did not develop to the same extent as the other stations south. A single coal siding with modest goods shed facility in corrugated iron on a brick base arranged alongside the track. The necessary weighbridge with attendant hut was installed at the entrance. The building pattern followed the variable style of the stations north of Rickmansworth, to Stoke Mandeville

For prospective modelmakers Albin J Reed's book *'Met & GC Joint Line an Observer's Notes'*, carries remarkable detail of the variety of application of colour schemes at the stations. Bearing in mind not only the original Joint Company's variations but what followed with London Transport, British Railways (London Midland Region), (Western Region), Network South East and now Chiltern Railways.

The last steam passenger working passed through the station on September 9, 1961. At that time the station was still using oil lamps! The yard closed on July 5, 1965 and its single siding was lifted in 1968. The signal box was demolished and burned on the site in 1969.

Not to dwell on the negative, the station now is neat and very attractive, presenting a positive approach to its users.

If one were to seek to use it one may be have one's curiosity aroused by some imposing and poignant sculptures in the area, now mostly grass, that was once a more formal garden. Stoke Mandeville has had its share in gardening triumphs in the past. The sculptures are the work of Sioban Coppinger with emblematic British Railways lions, but the most moving is of an apparent station porter holding a hoe in petrified gaze. This is the station porter-in-charge Bernard Carter aged 63, at the time of the work in October 1986 he lived at Verney Walk, Aylesbury. He had worked at this station for fifteen years. The statues had their days of fame as the British Rail's exhibit at the Chelsea Flower Show.

Statues in the past have largely been associated with the great and the good and it is to be applauded that the daily dedication of working people is duly recognised. At Gerrards Cross on the former GW & GC Joint line a robust railway navvy asserts his presence to passing trains. Here, Mr Carter gazes thoughtfully on.

Former Robinson 4-6-2 suburban tanks of the Great Central Railway now under the ownership of the LNER continuing to fulfil their role on the Aylesbury - Marylebone trains at Stoke Mandeville.

H C Casserley

Stoke Mandeville in the 1930s looking towards London. The 'down' platform buildings and canopy were demolished in 1964. The signal box can be seen in the distance facing the modest goods yard with its single siding. This was a time of exceptional travel poster art, although the poster facing, under the canopy, is too far away to be appreciated, it is a fine example of the genre, this one by J Littlejohns of 'Whitley Bay' c1929.

H C Casserley

Aylesbury - Baker Street train behind a Fairburn tank no 42253 of Neasden shed on July 26, 1958.

H C Casserley

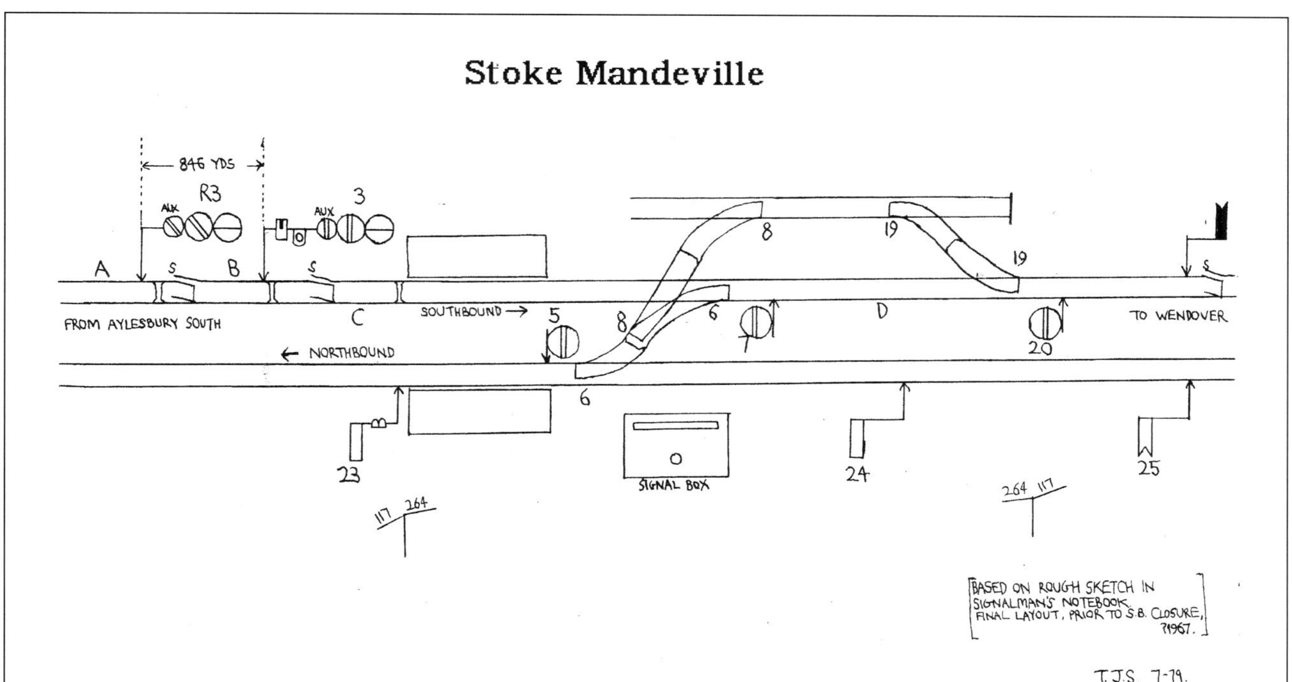

Signalling diagram for Stoke Mandeville

Tim Stevens

A Met H class 4-4-4 no 109 at Stoke Mandeville in the 1930's. Bunker first working was probably preferred for trains going south down the ruling gradient climbing in conventional position.

H C Casserley

One of the Robinson 4-6-2 tanks no 5170 working in the LNER days at Stoke Mandeville with a Marylebone train.

H C Casserley

Stoke Mandeville looking south towards Wendover on August 3, 1959. The modest goods yard is evident, the building along the single siding is the Goods Shed. The rubbish pit behind the buffer stops was eventually moved to allow lengthening of the platforms to accommodate eight-car trains. Note the 'scarfed' rail joint in the foreground.

Albin J Reed

A view looking north in the 1930's when the large stations signs were used near the oil lamp on the 'up' side.
H C Casserley

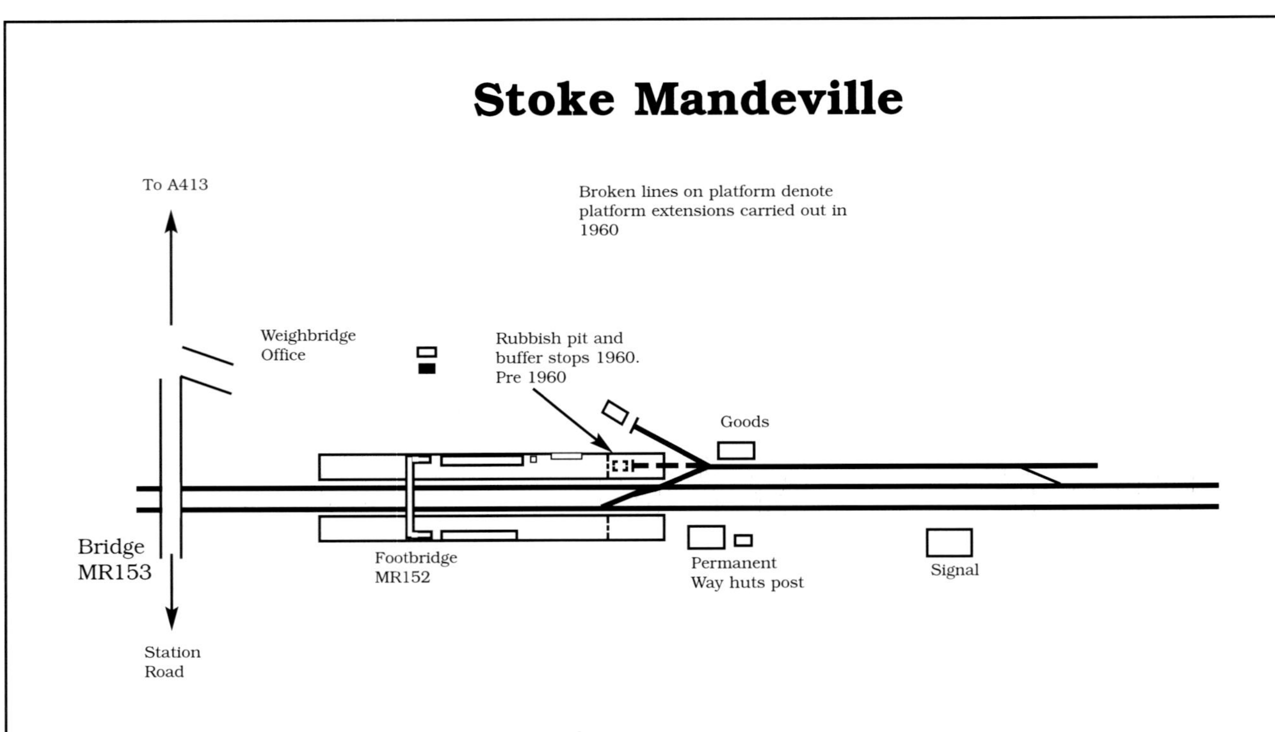

The station layout, largely unchanged from its opening in 1892

Albin J Reed

Stoke Mandeville in 1983 looking towards Aylesbury when the diesel multiple units ran the 'Chiltern Line' services to Marylebone.

Bill Simpson

One of the F class 0-6-2 tank engines that worked a great deal on the section between Wembley Park and Harrow, there were only four engines in the class. They were similar to the E class extended with an extra pair of driving wheesl which made them useful for their intended work of freight and coal trains.

R M Casserley Collection

One of the G class 0-6-4 tanks with a very varied goods train near Dutchlands summit in the early thirties still in the livery of the Metropolitan. The engine is believed to be no 96 'Charles Jones', the intriguing observation is the dark figure 3 on light ground oval plate above the buffer beam. Was this for train numbering, possibly?

H Gordon Tidy courtesy of the National Railway Museum

A Robinson 4-6-2 tank no 9800 on a train at Aylesbury in the 1940's, obviously having its water tanks replenished.
Alan Willmott

Chapter Ten
Aylesbury

The first station on the site was on the Wycombe Railway, part of the GWR, from Princes Risborough, who agreed to run the later Aylesbury & Buckingham Railway. In joint agreement they built the new station and instructed the engineer Frances Rummens to construct 'a good and direct access from County Hall and Market Square' to the station. This would be the first road connection to the railway station on this side of the town.

The first station of the Metropolitan Railway at Aylesbury was at the end of Brook Street, a short distance from the existing station, that was until that could be rebuilt to accommodate it. This was opened on September 1, 1892. It was a temporary timber structure for the first service of eight trains daily to and from Baker Street. The line from Rickmansworth had cost £350,000 or £22,000 per mile to reach there, some hard bargains with landowners had to be wrought.

At the opening the usual procession of Metropolitan hierarchy led by Sir Edward Watkin came for the celebratory opening banquet that took place in the Corn Exchange where it seemed that every person involved with railways in Buckinghamshire sat down to a towering feast which must have reduced their mobility somewhat when they arose. Whatever trials the railway officers endured abstinence was not one of them.

Watkin, rightly, made prominent reference to the ageing Sir Harry Verney, Bart. of Claydon House who, on rising to speak himself, pronounced his belief that from the outset he was certain that the progress to national prosperity was invested in the progress of railways. He

The station as rebuilt from the days of the arrival of the Metropolitan, seen here in the first decade of the twentieth century when it had become Joint to GCR and GWR. A Great Western train is entering the 'down' platform. The usual platform for lines to Princes Risborough seems very well stocked with coaches. The speeding GCR train came off just beyond and left of the rear coach of the GWR train.

S G Payne

mentioned his meeting with George Stephenson who spoke of the pathway north along the route now taken by the Metropolitan being ideal. From his energies in founding the Buckinghamshire Railway (1846 - 1890). Sir Harry had championed railways and benefactions for Bucks for forty-four years.

A few years later on Thursday, March 9, 1899, shortly after 4 pm the first train started from Marylebone station as Mr Ritchie, President of the Board of Trade pulled a lever to start it. Previous to this happening three special trains had brought visitors from the north including Lady Verney who had travelled from Sheffield and alighted at Aylesbury. This train was due at Aylesbury at 12.22 but due to an axle running hot did not arrive until 1 pm. Sir Edmund Verney attended the banquet at Marylebone. There must have been some raised eyebrows for those not yet aware that the London Extension had cost the GCR £12 million with £4 million on the London section. It would take much to recover this sum and in all probability, never was.

The sharp curve at Aylesbury had been the bane of the GCR, who looked to essential fast running on their line.

Regrettably it seems to be the dilemma of all human failing that potential hazards have to be brought to prominence through tragedy. For the families involved of the three men killed it was tragedy enough. The potential for it to have been far worse, had it been a full heavy passenger train instead of a newspaper and parcels train, was nothing short of providential.

This was the accident that ocurred at 3.40 am on Friday morning, December 23, 1904. The train was the 2.45 am from Marylebone. As it rounded the tight curve then ran into the turnout line of opposing points, the locomotive was unable to withstand the reverse forces and left the track at speed, falling across the down platform, whilst the vehicles behind were thrown against the brickwork of the platform. The effect of the forces involved can be realised as the locomotive smashed apart. It defies imagination to visualise the violent movement of force that had been driving the train north, suddenly, and completely out of control. The only vehicle to escape this disintegration was the guard's van. Providence once more that it should happen when the platforms would be largely deserted, a few hours later they would have been crowded with Christmas travellers.

As the smash took place another train was speeding south, the 10.20 pm from Manchester. The signalman in the north box, Keedle, acted with commendable composure and threw all his signals to danger. This reduced the speed of the train in time. It is a measure of the force of the impact of the smash to think that the driver of this second train heard it above the roar of his own engine and was exerting all force that he could to bring it to a standstill. Not completely successful, but enough not to cause further injury. What it did do, which again was a miti-

The junction viewed south of the station where the excessive curve on the Metropolitan & GCR Joint (left) was too severe for fast running which caused the accident of December 1904. The signalbox is in the orginal position, this was moved when the curve was eased out and the point arrangement was changed.

S G Payne

gating to catastrophe was to dislodge wreckage so that some of those injured could extricate themselves from it.

On the initial train, sadly, driver Joseph Barnshaw of Openshaw Gorton, Manchester was thrown with great force from his engine and was found lying on the other side of the 'down' platform. He was removed to the Royal Bucks Hospital where his physical injuries with severe scalding were so severe, he died at 12.30 pm on the following day, Saturday. His fireman George Masters, also of Openshaw, Manchester was found to be dead at the scene. Thomas Masters, dining car attendant was sleeping in the train when violently awoken. Although he became seriously trapped he was aided to escape by the collision of the second train. At the Royal Bucks it was found that his injuries were not life threatening.

Two other railway officers travelling as passengers were killed, Daniel Somers a driver and Joseph Stanton a fireman both from Neasden. Guard Chas Blackmore of Dog Lane, Neasden was thrown into bushes by the side of the line and had cuts and bruises. A porter called Cooper who was with him escaped with a cut head and badly shaken.

It must have been a chilling scene in a number of respects as it was foggy with a heavy frost. Trying to pierce the gloom with a ring of bright kerosene lights with shouts of rescuers and workers. The rumble of moving wreckage as three steam cranes worked, exhausting spouts of quickly condensing steam. Everywhere there were piles of newspapers and thousands of ill fated Christmas presents. General Manager of the Metropolitan Railway Mr A C Ellis was soon present with the Operating Superintendent Mr H B Palmer, with many other officials of the Joint Committee. It was not until the first gloomy daylight at eight o' clock that the first body was recovered.

Trains going north and south were halted beyond the station and passengers had to walk from and to them. Any mails and newspapers that had survived the smash were placed in a train and continued northwards.

The engine no 1040 was eventually totally scrapped.

It was just after 7 o'clock of Friday evening that the 'up' line was cleared and made available for cautious use for trains to London. The obvious conclusion and timely warning to the Joint Committee was that something had to be done about the south curve.

Steam workings south of Aylesbury were taken over from the LPTB by the LNER in 1938. These included considerable goods workings from Aylesbury, Watford, Chesham and Uxbridge.

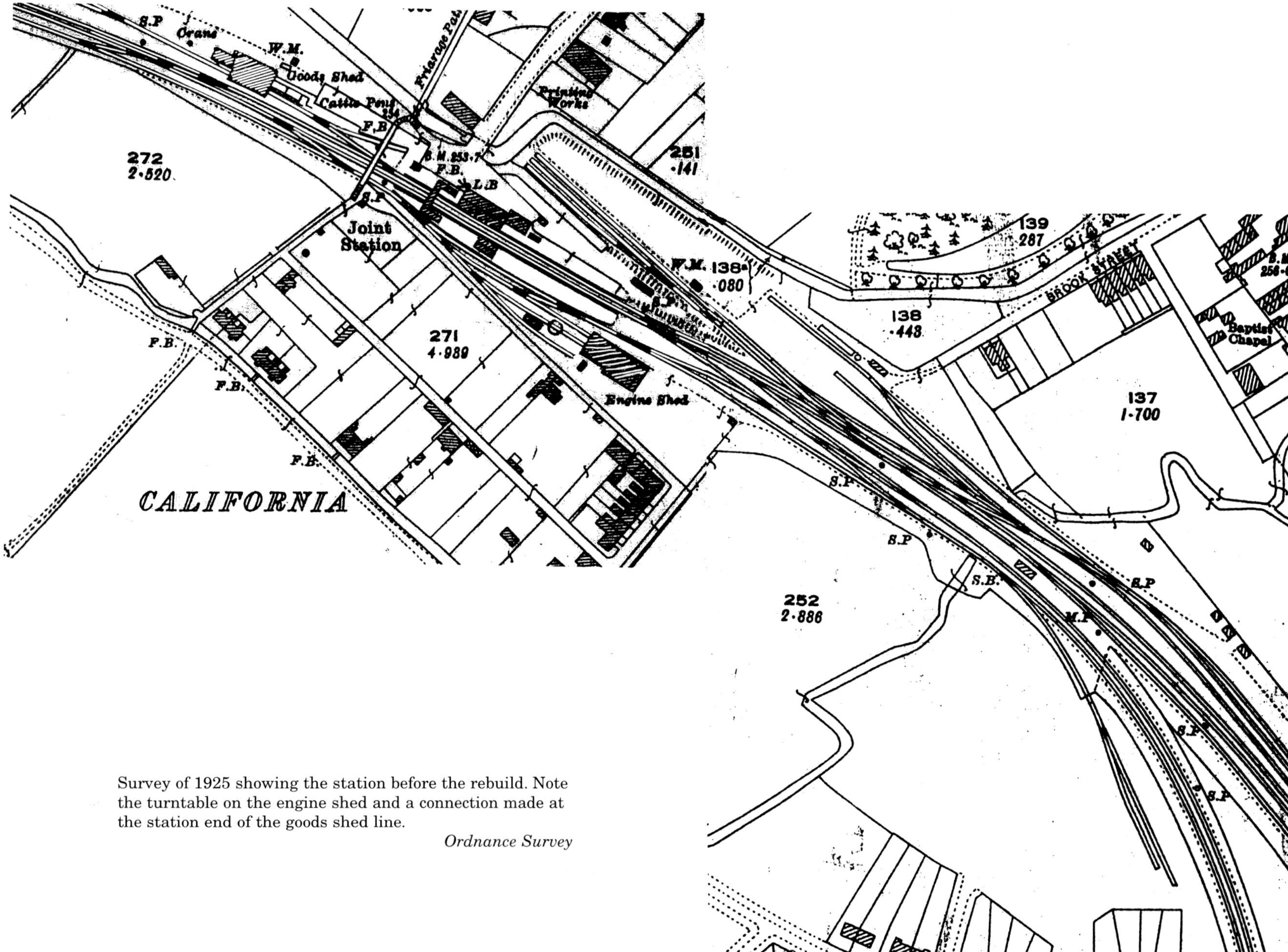

Survey of 1925 showing the station before the rebuild. Note the turntable on the engine shed and a connection made at the station end of the goods shed line.

Ordnance Survey

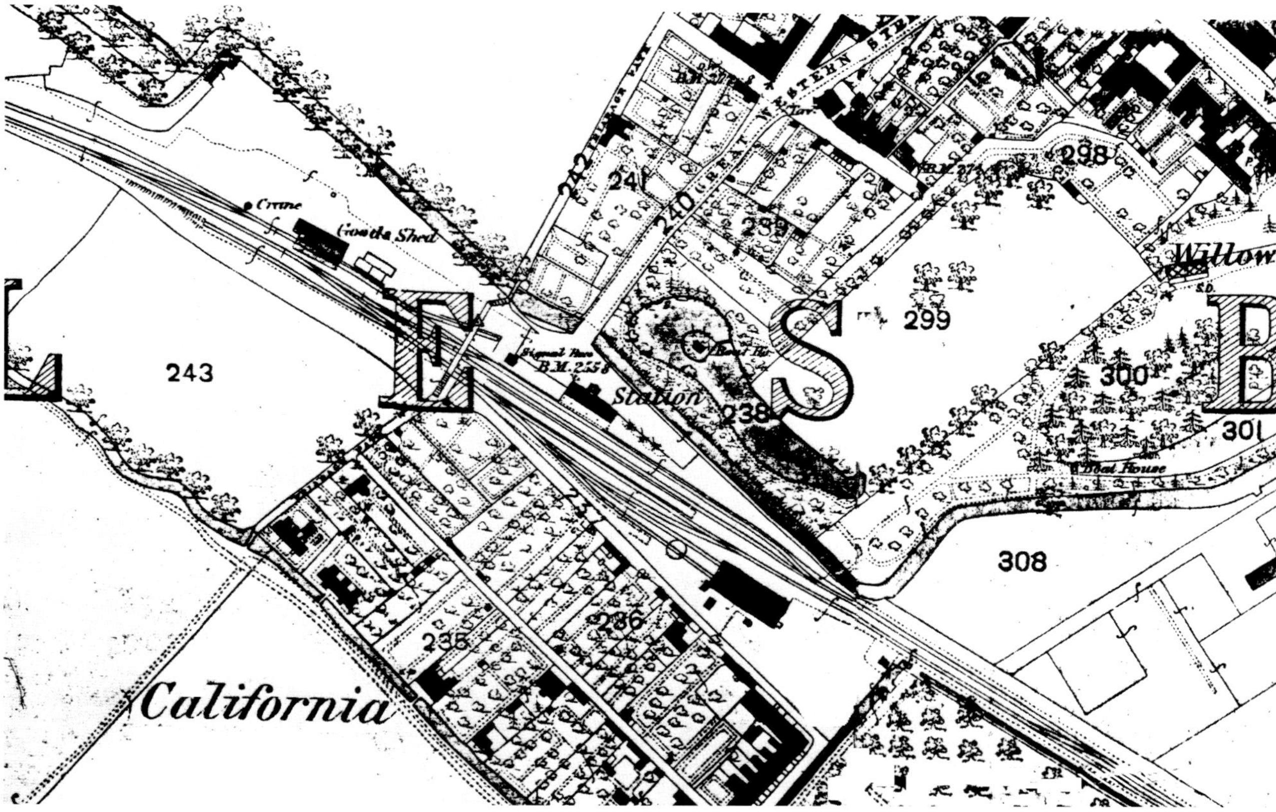

Aylesbury railway station in 1883, originally a broad gauge terminus of the Wycombe Railway from Maidenhead, High Wycombe and Princes Risborough. It became a through station with the extension north to Verney Junction in 1868. It became part of the Metropolitan Railway in 1891 when it was expanded further to accept main line expressess of the GCR after 1899. The station buildings are quite modest, similar the photograph on page 124, the down platform had not yet received the building seen there. The original broad gauge goods shed was sited much closer to the station, this was built anew further north and the original base was used for cattle pens.

Ordnance Survey

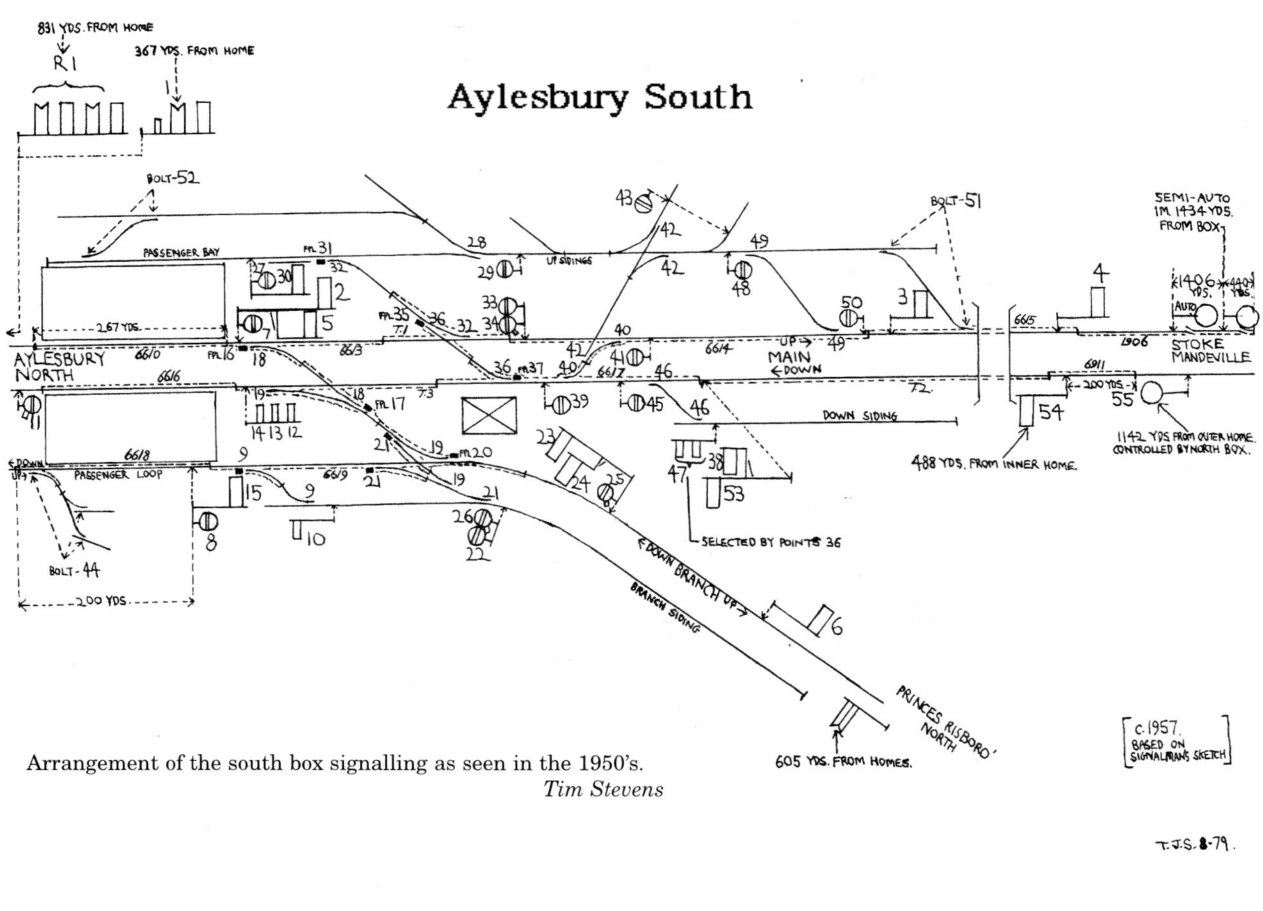

Arrangement of the south box signalling as seen in the 1950's.

Tim Stevens

Aylesbury station approach in 1934, good selection of period road vehicles with the one time very popular motorcycle combination seen on the right. The new station was completed and opened in 1926 from the drawings of Charles J Brown the LNER engineer. The contractors for the project were John Wilmott & Sons (Hitchin) Ltd, including the goods yard requirement of moving the Goods Shed and building of cattle pens which cost £61,114. To this the Metropolitan subscribed one quarter.

London's Transport Museum

London's Transport Museum

Looking north at Aylesbury in 1934, as a station at its high point in terms of structures. The Locomotive engine shed on the left and the coal yard sidings on the right. Inset a closer view of the station area and signalbox beyond.

Aylesbury station before the rebuilding of 1925-26 looking south. The problem curve and points that required a slow down at the station can be seen beyond the platform end. Note the signalbox, this owes more to GCR design than Metropolitan.

Leicestershire County Council

The view looking north at the same time, a comprehensive view of the GWR and A&BR station before it was rebuilt as a Met&GCR GWR Joint station. The building beyond the end of the 'up' platform was a small frame box to operate points in the yard. The man standing in the six foot appears to be waiting to apply lubrication. Not a place to dwell unattentively!

Leicestershire County Council

Work at Aylesbury, probably after the terrible train smash of December 1904, alterations to the curve at the south end of the station were not as rapid as required. The arrangement is still extant on the plans of 1906. It seems that the extensive rebuilding of the lines south to make the main line of the Met&GCR in engineering preference to the GWR branch did not come until the early 1920's and may have been due more to the LNER, who realigned the track at Quainton. Note the cabless A class tank no 7 in the background and the old Met coach probably of the Brown Marshall stock.

Authors Collection

The derailment smash of December 1904, both locomotives can be seen, the one on its side probably the original train engine, whilst the engine that subsequently hit the wreckage can be seen upright. Thousands of parcels of Christmas presents were scattered over a wide area.

Authors Collection

One of the magnificent Robinson Atlantics no 6090 seen in LNER days, June 22, 1935 on a Marylebone train.

H C Casserley

Metropolitan complete train with H class 4-4-4 no 103 in the passenger bay at Aylesbury probably an early morning train to Baker Street in the 1920's.

R K Blencowe

View north in the 1940's showing the complete assembly of railway structures with the later goods shed and the Aylesbury north signal box.

A A Edser

The view north some forty years later in the early 1980's, on the right are the remains of the original broad gauge goods shed that was later utilised as the cattle dock. All of this has now been removed and the area has been developed.

Bill Simpson

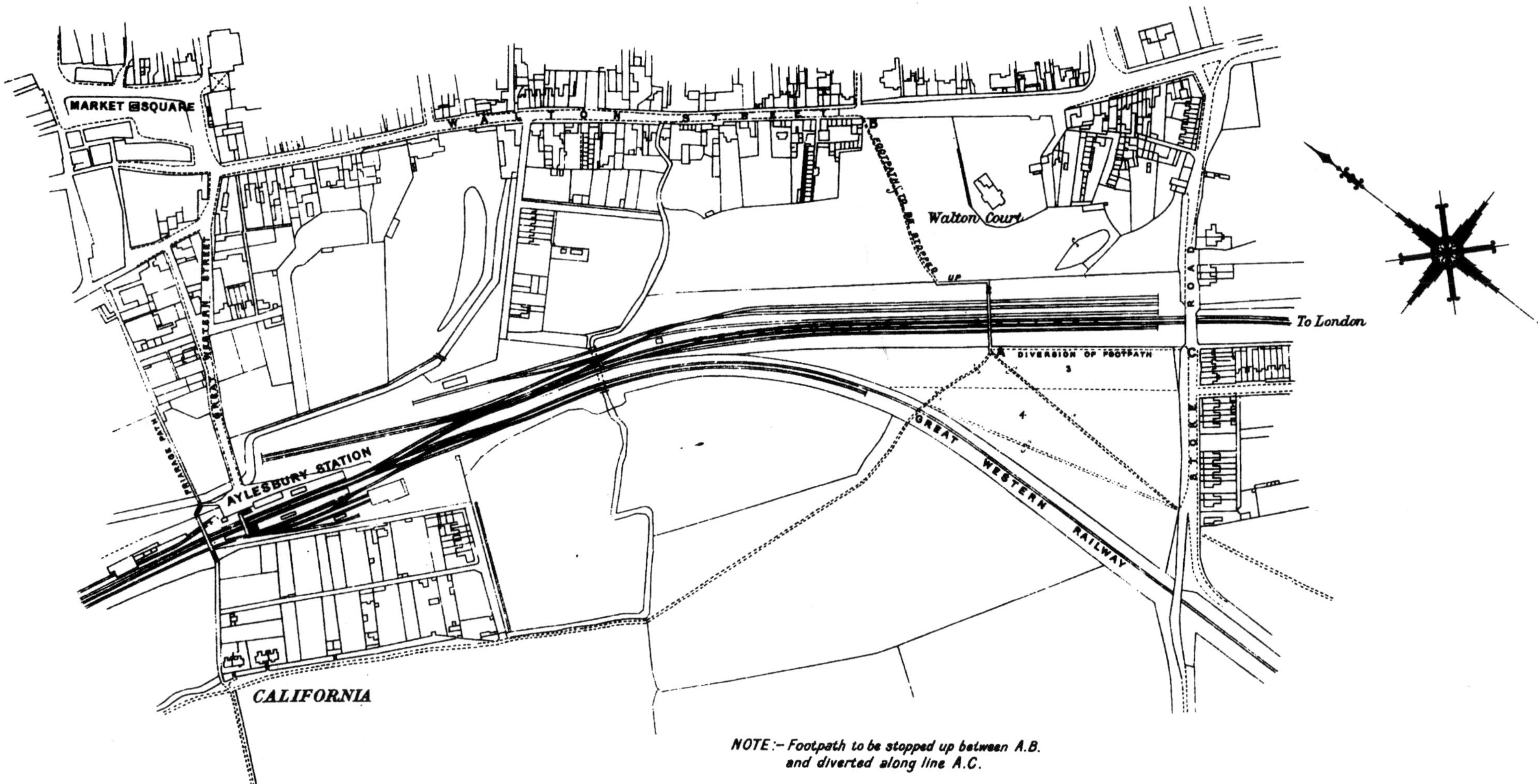

Plans of 1906 intended for the diversion of the footpath that passed over the railway on a bridge. This would be for the work of removing the offending junction which can be seen here close to the station where the Met & GC Joint lines join the GWR on something of a tangent. Apart from this work, further sidings accommodation would be needed. To do this the former company had the advantage of utilising the nearby road bridge carrying the Stoke Road over the railway. Note the plans show the early station building of the GWR, eventually totally replaced in 1925-26. Work on the junction was undertaken in 1907. It appears on this plan that the former GWR locomotive shed has no turntable, nor a station side connection with the goods shed. This likely to be an omission of the draughtsman as both of these facilities existed on the 1883 survey and again on the 1925 survey.

Aylesbury Public Archives, Buckinghamshire Centre for Local Studies

AYLESBURY AND BUCKINGHAM SECTION.

LEAVE.	A.M.	A.M.	A.M.	P.M.	
AYLESBURY	7 50	10 0	12 0	3 50	...
Quainton Road	8 5	1015	1215	4 5	...
Grandborough Road	8 15	1025	1225	4 15	...
Winslow Road	8 20	1030	1230	4 20	...
Verney Junction ... arrive	8 25	1035	1235	4 25	...
Ditto ... depart for Oxford	8 40	1038	2 16	4 41	...
Ditto ... depart for Banbury	8 51	1045	1257	4 55	...
Ditto ... depart for Bletchley	8 31	1038	1245	5 30	...
Bicester ... arrive	9 12	1059	2 36	5 8	...
Oxford ... ,,	9 39	1125	3 0	5 31	...
Padbury ... ,,	8 58	1052	1 4	5 2	...
Buckingham ... ,,	9 5	1059	1 9	5 9	...
Fulwell and Westbury ,,	9 15	1110	1 19	5 16	...
Brackley ... ,,	9 22	1119	1 25	5 22	...
Farthinghoe ... ,,	9 34	...	1 36	5 37	...
Banbury ... ,,	9 48	...	1 47	5 47	...
Winslow ... ,,	8 35	1043	1250	5 26	...
Bletchley ... ,,	8 54	1058	1 6	5 45	...
Bedford ... arrive	9 33	1230	2 33	7 6	...

LEAVE.	A.M.	A.M.	A.M.	A.M.	P.M.
Bedford	...	...	8 51	1028	2 47
Bletchley	...	...	1015	1230	4 25
Winslow	...	...	1030	1246	4 43
Verney Junction ... arrive	...	...	1036	1252	4 52
Oxford ... depart for Aylesbury	...	8 0	9 50	12 5	4 45
Bicester ... ,,	...	8 22	1014	1228	5 5
Verney Junction ... arrive	...	8 34	1036	1245	5 27
Banbury ... depart for Aylesbury	7 15	8 0	9 50	...	4 35
Farthinghoe ... ,,	7 23	...	9 59	...	4 42
Brackley ... ,,	7 36	8 16	1011	...	4 55
Fulwell and Westbury ... ,,	7 45	...	1018	...	5 1
Buckingham ... ,,	7 57	8 32	1028	...	5 10
Padbury ... ,,	8 4	..	1035	...	5 16
Verney Junction ... arrive	8 10	8 40	1040	...	5 20
Ditto depart for Aylesbury	...	8 45	1045	1255	5 32
Winslow Road	...	8 48	1048	1258	5 35
Grandborough Road ... arrive	...	8 53	1053	1 3	5 39
Quainton Road ... ,,	...	9 5	11 5	1 15	5 50
AYLESBURY ... ,,	...	9 17	1120	1 30	6 5

Aylesbury & Buckingham Railway, now part of the Metropolitan in September 1892, showing connnections on the Oxford to Cambridge line and branch to Banbury.

METROPOLITAN RAILWAY

DOWN TRAINS.

	WEEK DAYS.													SUNDAYS.							
	A.M	A.M	A.M	A.M	A.M	P.M	P.M	P.M	P.M	P.M	P.M	P.M	P.M	A.M	A.M	P.M	P.M	P.M	P.M	P.M	P.M
BAKER STREET ... dep.	6 19	7 9	7 27	9 27	1127	1 27	2 27	3 27	5 27	6 29	7 27	9 27	1140	8 47	9 47	1 16	3 16	5 16	7 16	8 16	9 16
St. John's Wood Road	6 22	7 12	...	...	...	...	...	...	...	6 32	...	...	1152	8 50	9 50	1 19	3 19	5 19	7 19	8 19	9 19
Marlborough Road	6 24	7 14	...	...	...	...	...	...	...	6 34	...	...	1154	8 52	9 52	1 21	3 21	5 21	7 21	8 21	9 21
Swiss Cottage	6 26	7 16	...	...	...	...		...	...	6 36	...	...	1156	8 54	9 54	1 23	3 23	5 23	7 23	8 23	9 23
Finchley Road	6 28	7 18	...	...	...	...		...	...	6 38	...	...	1158	8 56	9 56	1 25	3 25	5 25	7 25	8 25	9 25
West Hampstead	6 30	7 20	...	...	...	...		...	...	6 40	...	...	12 0	8 58	9 58	1 27	3 27	5 27	7 27	8 27	9 27
Kilburn-Brondesbury	6 32	7 22	...	...	...	...		...	...	6 42	...	...	12 2	9 0	10 0	1 29	3 29	5 29	7 29	8 29	9 29
WILLESDEN GREEN	6 35	7 25	7 39	9 39	1139	1 39	*Sats. only.*	3 39	5 39	6 45	7 39	9 39	12 5	9 2	10 2	1 32	3 32	5 32	7 32	8 32	9 32
Kingsbury-Neasden	6 45	7 30	...	...	...	...	...	...	...	6 48	...	...	12 8	9 5	10 5	1 35	3 35	5 35	7 35	8 35	9 35
Harrow-on-the-Hill	6 53	7 38	7 48	9 48	1148	1 48	2 48	3 48	5 48	6 56	7 48	9 48	1216	9 13	1013	1 43	3 43	5 43	7 43	1 43	9 43
Pinner	6 58	7 43	7 53	9 53	1153	1 53	2 53	3 53	5 53	7 1	7 53	9 53	1221	9 18	1018	1 48	3 48	5 48	7 48	8 48	9 48
Northwood	7 3	7 48	7 58	9 58	1158	1 58	2 58	3 58	5 58	7 6	7 58	9 58	1226	9 23	1023	1 53	3 53	5 53	5 53	8 53	9 53
Rickmansworth	7 10	7 55	8 5	10 5	12 5	2 5	3 5	4 5	6 5	7 13	8 5	10 5	1233	9 30	1030	2 0	4 0	6 0	8 0	9 0	10 0
Chorley Wood	7 16	8 1	8 11	1011	1211	2 11	3 11	4 11	6 11	7 19	8 11	1011	1239	9 36	1036	2 6	4 6	6 6	8 6	9 6	10 6
Chalfont Road	7 22	8 7	8 17	1017	1217	2 17	3 17	4 17	6 17	7 25	8 17	1017	1245	9 42	1042	2 12	4 12	6 12	8 12	9 12	1012
CHESHAM ... arr.	7 31	8 16	8 27	1027	1227	2 27	3 27	4 27	6 27	7 34	8 27	1028	1254	9 51	1051	2 21	4 21	6 21	8 21	9 21	1021
Amersham	...	...	8 22	1022	1222	2 22	...	4 22	6 22	...	8 22	1024	*Pinner to Chesham Wed only.*	...	1049	2 19	...	6 19	...	9 19	...
Great Missenden	...	...	8 32	1032	1232	2 32	...	4 32	6 32	...	8 32	1034		...	1059	2 29	...	6 29	...	9 29	...
Wendover	...	...	8 41	1041	1241	2 41	...	4 41	6 41	...	8 41	1043		...	11 8	2 38	...	6 38	...	9 38	...
Stoke Mandeville	...	...	8 46	1046	1246	2 46	...	4 46	6 46	...	8 46	1048		...	1113	2 43	...	6 43	...	9 43	...
AYLESBURY ... arr.	...	...	8 52	1052	1252	2 52	...	4 52	6 52	...	8 52	1054		..	1118	2 48	...	6 48	...	9 48	...
,, depart for Verney	7 50	...	10 0	12 0	..	3 50	...	...	...	...	...	...		...	...	...	...	...	...	...	...
Quainton Road	8 5	..	1015	1215	...	4 5	...	...	...	...	...	...		...	...	...	...	...	...	...	...
Grandborough Road	8 15	..	1025	1225	...	4 15	...	...	...	...	...	...		..	...	...	...	...	...	...	...
Winslow Road	8 20	...	1030	1230	..	4 20	...	...	...	...	...	...		..	...	...	...	...	...	...	...
VERNEY JUNCTION arr.	8 25	...	1035	1235	...	4 25	...	...	...	...	...	...		..	...	...	...	...	...	...	...

UP TRAINS.

	WEEK DAYS.													SUNDAYS.							
	A.M	A.M	A.M	A.M	A.M	P.M	P.M	P.M	P.M	P.M	P.M	P.M	P.M	A.M	P.M	P.M	P.M	P.M	P.M	P.M	P.M
VERNEY JUNCTION dep.	...	...	8 45	1045	...	1255	...	...	5 32	...	...	...	...	...	...	...	...	...	...	...	...
Winslow Road	...	...	8 48	1048	...	1258	...	...	5 35	...	...	...	...	...	...	...	...	...	...	...	...
Grandborough Road	...	...	8 53	1053	...	1 3	...	...	5 39	...	...	...	...	...	...	...	...	...	...	...	...
Quainton Road	...	...	9 5	11 5	...	1 15	...	...	5 50	...	...	...	...	...	...	...	...	...	...	...	...
AYLESBURY ... arr.	...	...	9 17	1120	..	1 30	...	...	6 5	...	...	...	...	...	...	...	...	...	...	...	...
AYLESBURY ... dep	7 13	...	9 23	1123	1 23	3 23	*Sats. only.*	5 23	7 23	...	9 23	...	...	9 32	1222	...	4 22	...	8 22	...	...
Stoke Mandeville	7 19	...	9 29	1129	1 29	3 29		5 29	7 29	...	9 29	...	..	9 38	1228	...	4 28	...	8 28	...	..
Wendover	7 25	...	9 35	1135	1 35	3 35		5 35	7 35	...	9 35	...	...	9 43	1233	...	4 33	...	8 33	...	...
Great Missenden	7 34	...	9 44	1144	1 44	3 44		5 44	7 44	...	9 44	...	...	9 52	1242	...	4 42	...	8 42	...	...
Amersham	7 44	..	9 54	1154	1 54	3 54		5 54	7 54	...	9 54	...	...	10 2	1252	...	4 52	...	8 52	...	...
CHESHAM ... dep.	7 38	8 43	9 48	1148	1 48	3 48	4 0	5 48	7 48	9 0	9 48	1040	..	9 59	1249	2 49	4 49	6 49	8 53	9 49	1029
Chalfont Road	7 51	8 53	10 1	12 1	2 1	4 1	4 11	6 1	8 1	9 11	10 1	1051	..	1010	1 0	3 0	5 0	7 0	9 4	10 0	1040
Chorley Wood	7 55	8 57	10 5	12 5	2 5	4 5	4 15	6 5	8 5	9 15	10 5	1055	..	1014	1 4	3 4	5 4	7 4	9 8	10 4	1044
Rickmansworth	8 0	9 2	1010	1210	2 10	4 10	4 20	6 10	8 10	9 20	1010	1120	...	1019	1 9	3 9	5 9	7 9	9 13	10 9	1049
Northwood	8 7	9 9	1017	1217	2 17	4 17	4 27	6 17	8 17	9 27	1017	1127	...	1026	1 16	3 16	5 16	7 16	9 20	1016	1056
Pinner	8 12	9 13	1022	1222	2 22	4 22	4 32	6 22	8 22	2 32	1022	1132	..	1031	1 21	3 21	5 21	7 21	9 25	1021	11 1
Harrow-on-the-Hill	8 17	9 18	1027	1227	2 27	4 27	4 37	6 27	8 27	9 37	1027	1137	...	1036	1 26	3 26	5 26	7 26	9 30	1026	11 6
Kingsbury-Neasden	...	...	...	...	...	...	4 45	...	...	9 45	...	1145	...	1044	1 34	3 34	5 34	7 34	9 38	1034	1114
WILLESDEN GREEN	8 27	...	1037	1237	2 37	4 37	4 49	6 37	8 37	9 49	1037	1149	...	1048	1 38	3 38	5 38	7 38	9 42	1038	...
Kilburn-Brondesbury	...	...	...	...	...	...	4 51	...	...	9 51	...	1151	...	1050	1 40	3 40	5 40	7 40	9 44	1040	...
West Hampstead	...	...	...	...	...	...	4 54	...	...	9 54	...	1154	...	1053	1 43	3 43	5 43	7 43	9 47	1043	...
Finchley Road	...	9 30	...	...	...	4 42	4 56	6 42	...	9 56	...	1156	...	1055	1 45	3 45	5 45	7 45	9 49	1045	...
Swiss Cottage	...	...	...	...	...	...	4 58	...	...	9 58	...	1158	...	1057	1 47	3 47	5 47	7 47	9 51	1047	...
Marlborough Road	...	...	...	...	...	...	5 0	...	...	10 0	...	12 0	..	1059	1 49	3 49	5 49	7 49	9 53	1049	...
St. John's Wood Road	...	...	...	...	...	...	5 2	...	...	10 2	...	12 2	...	11 1	1 51	3 51	5 51	7 51	9 55	1051	...
BAKER STREET ... arr.	8 37	9 37	1047	1247	2 47	4 48	5 5	6 48	8 47	10 5	1047	12 5	...	11 4	1 54	3 54	5 54	7 54	9 58	1054	...

Timetable for the Metropolitan Railway for September 1892 after the opening of the Metropolitan station at Aylesbury.

A Thompson B1 Class 4-6-0 no 1299 in Aylesbury with the 'South Yorkshireman' The 'South Yorkshireman' had an interesting past. It was due to the Huddersfield Chamber of Commerce in 1884 needing a direct rail connection to London. This commenced on a route from Bradford to Huddersfield, Sheffield, Retford and Kings Cross. With the opening of the Great Central main line in 1899 the train was then routed via Nottingham and Leicester to Marylebone. It only received the name in the early British Railways period. The engine is in some transition as it has the LNER number and is in Apple Green but carries the 'British Railways' name on the tender. This is in 1948 when it was a Leicester engine. It was withdrawn in 1965 and scrapped by Cohen at Ickle.

Jack Turner Collection

The magnificent K class 2-6-4 tank of the Metropolitan Railway undertaking its intended role by hauling a goods train at Aylesbury in the 1920's. The names on the private owners wagons are Albert Fisher, London and Melroy & Co, London. An interesting building to those familiar with Aylesbury will be the Bull's Head Hotel on higher ground in the distance.

R K Blencowe

An H class 4-4-4 no 110 in the bay at Aylesbury station on April 8, 1933.

H C Casserley

The steam locomotive shed at Aylesbury Joint station in the late 1950's. Originally it would have been a broad gauge shed at the end of the branch from Princes Risborough which probably sufficed on this site. However, with the arrival of the Metropolitan the site would take some modification. An example of this was the less than adequate water tower above the coaling stage that was replaced by the larger one at the side of the shed providing a head of water to the columns. As a GWR shed it was a sub shed of Slough and had a locomotive supplied by Banbury to work the Princes Risborough to Aylesbury service. It became a sub shed to Neasden (34E) also which is the way things remained until closure in the mid 1960's. The engine is one of the Fairburn tanks probably on the Aylesbury - Rickmansworth service.

Author's Collection

One of the Met K class no 111 shunting the yard at Aylesbury, in the distance on the right, is one of the Pullman cars stored on a siding.

R K Blencowe / Lens of Sutton

A through working to Paddington, March 15, 1930, behind a Great Western 2-6-2 tank no 2222 which provided an alternative to the service to Baker Street from the station. Note the grounded old Metropolitan coach body alongside.

H C Casserley

Metropolitan Pullman cars details

Car serial names 'Galatea' 'Mayflower'
No of cars - 2
Date entered service 1909
Weight unloaded 29 tons
Number of seats: smoking 19
Non smoking none
Lights: number 26, 24 volts per lamp, watts 15
Heaters: number 10 in two circuits, volts per heater 120, watts 360, kilowatts 3.6 per car
Axle journals; dia $4^1/_2$", length 9"
Axle bearing load, new bearing 458lbs, per sqaure inch 201lbs
Wheel diameter 3' x $4^5/_8$
Brake gear type: vacuum
No of cylinders 2
Cylinder diameter 21"
Braking force 106%wt of car, 69000lbs
Type of couplings, screw couplings

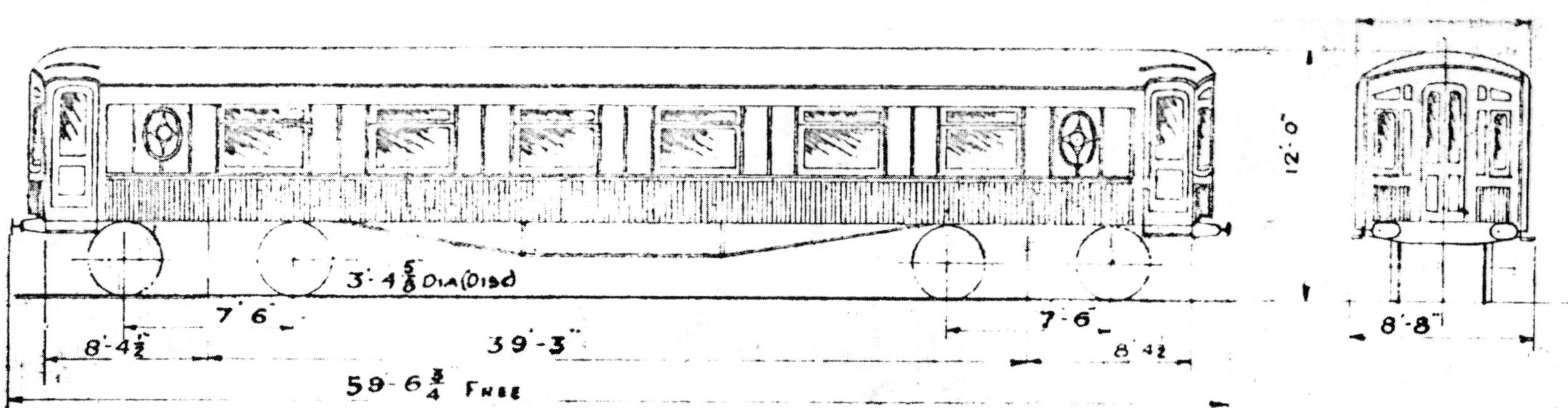

Two first class Pullman cars were introduced on the Metropolitan to run on the outer suburban business trains, by this meaning from Liverpool Street to Verney Junction and to Chesham. This was introduced in 1910. Morning trains returning in the early evening. They also ran in a midnight theatre train from Baker Street to Aylesbury which sounds like a perfect conclusion to an evening out in the city. The images of glistening Pullmans standing in remote Buckinghamshire countryside was to be short lived however. The service was suspended during the first world war and on return to go no further than Aylesbury. They were later reduced from their striking chocolate and cream livery to red in the 1930's, as the car 'Mayflower' seen here on the siding at Aylesbury on May 2, 1936.

H C Casserley

Aylesbury in the early 1980's with class 25 coming down from the good shed. Access to and from the station is through the main building here, which has now been been closed with the modification carried out in recent years of new ticket hall. Semaphore platform starter has now gone with new electric signalling. The footbridge has also been rebuilt.

Bill Simpson

August 1966 and diesel trains are very much in evidence with the olive green diesel multiple unit train on platform 2. When electrification reached Amersham the services between there and Aylesbury were operated as a shuttle using the dmu's. Others working through to Marylebone. The empty steam shed is portent that in two years time steam traction would cease on British Railway's lines altogether, note the GWR water column.

RAS Marketing

The view south on July 23, 1955 with a British Railways 2-6-4 Standard tank no 80117 on a Baker Street train, which would of course change engines at Rickmansworth. Just a glimpse of B1 4-6-0 no 60961 on the right which would be bound for Marylebone.

H C Casserley

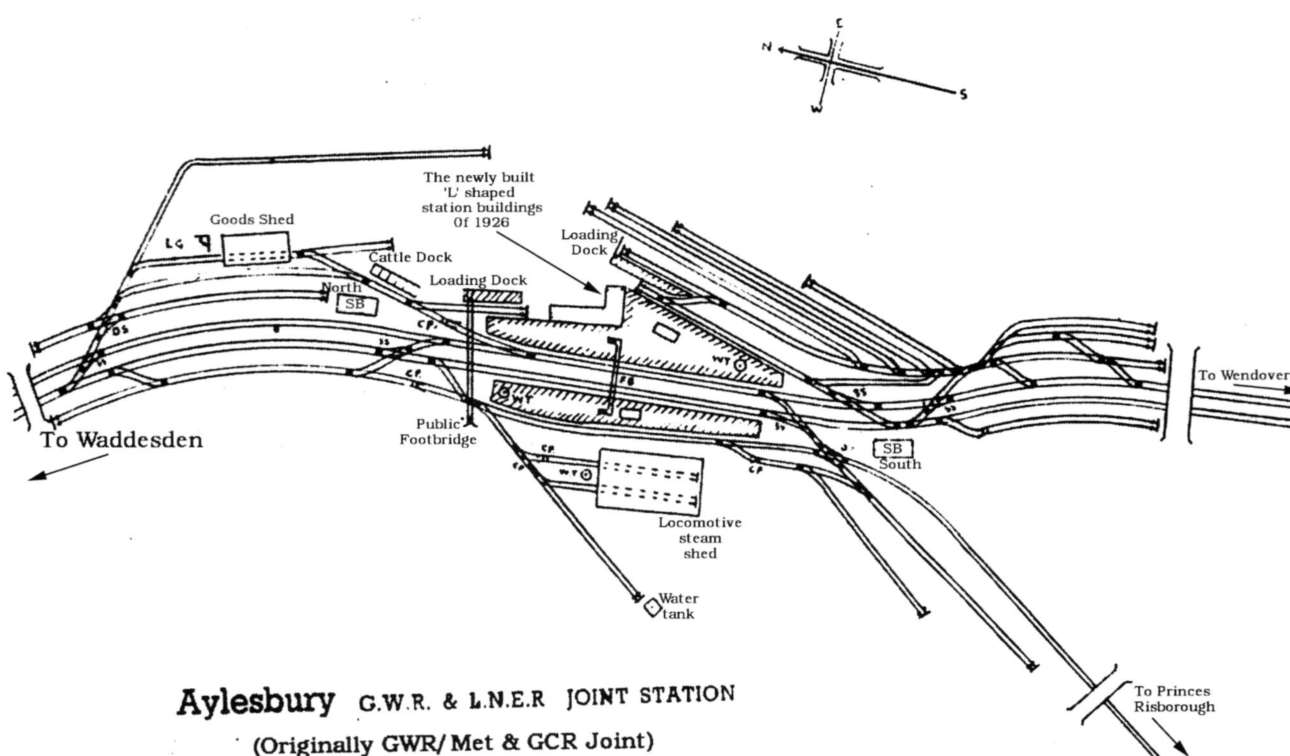

Aylesbury Met & LNER Joint in its final form. The signalbox south was moved in the complete realignment of 1925 to make the Joint lines the main route and the original GWR line the branch.

Steam stopping trains and expresses ran beyond Aylesbury by GCR, later LNER with British Railways Eastern Region. It was handed over to the London Midland Region during its final years running to Nottingham only. It ended in two stages of closure, 1963 and 1966. This view September 1, 1966.

K C H Fairey

Early days of British Railways in the 1950's with 69829 a class A5 4-6-2 tank, a Robinson Great Central Railway design.

Jack Turner

One of the GWR 2-6-2 tanks no 3906 alongside the coaling stage at Aylesbury on March 15, 1930.

H C Casserley

To those so inclined there were few pleasures greater than the enthusiasts excursions in the days when much of the original railway was still evident. Here at Aylesbury on August 13, 1966 such an excursion has called and they are able to examine the steam shed that was still standing. This was 150ft x 33ft with offices and stores building of 80ft x 15ft. It was brick built with a saw-tooth roof pattern glazed for northern light. At this time the station was known as Aylesbury Town, a name remaining from the days of the Aylesbury High Street on the Cheddington branch.

H C Casserley

The view early 1980's with class 25 shunting. The passenger bay obviously still in use and the far parcels vans stored on the former coal yard sidings. All of this is now the station car park.

BIll Simpson

Aylesbury on September 1, 1966 looking towards London. A dmu waits in the bay whilst a class 25 shunts vans in the adjoining yard. A few days later the former Great Central main line beyond Aylesbury was closed and the track rapidly removed.

K Fairey

Dreadnought coach number 496 now lettered in Johnston's famous new London Transport typeface. This is in the bay at Aylesbury on May 2, 1936.

H C Casserley

What became the final image of the once proud GCR main line. With the line passing from the administration of the ER to LMR in the early sixties trains from Marylebone to the north became commonly Stanier Black Fives, in this case 44540 with maroon coaches. The train is passing the Aylesbury South signal box on September 1, 1966.

K C H Fairey

AYLESBURY - AMERSHAM - HARROW - LONDON — **Metropolitan Line Table 1**

All trains third class only except where otherwise stated.

MONDAY to FRIDAY

No. 1.																						
AYLESBURY	....	....	6 6	....	6 35	....	6 51	....	....	....	7 11	....	7 25	....	7 38	....	....	....	7 51	....	8 3	....
STOKE MAND'VILLE	..	..	6 13	..	6 42	..	6 58	..	..	..	7 18	..	7 32	..	..	..	..	..	7 58	..	8 10	..
WENDOVER	....	....	6 20	....	6 49	....	7 5	....	....	....	7 25	....	7 39	....	7 50	....	....	....	8 5	....	8 17	....
Great Missenden	..	..	6 30	..	6 59	..	7 15	..	..	..	7 35	..	7 49	..	..	..	..	..	8 15	..	8 27	..
Amersham	....	....	6 40	....	7 9	....	7 25	....	....	....	7 45	....	8 0	....	8 7	....	....	....	8 25	....	8 37	....
Chesham dep.	5 41	..	6 34	..	7 3	..	..	..	7 29	..	..	..	7 54	..	..	..	8 9	..	..	..	..	..
Chalfont & Latimer	5 50	....	6 45	....	7 14	....	7 30	....	7 39	....	7 50	....	8 5	....	8 12	....	8 19	....	8 31	....	8 42	....
Chorley Wood	5 54	..	6 49	..	7 18	..	7 34	..	7 43	..	7 54	..	..	..	8 16	..	8 23	..	8 35	..	8 46	..
Rickmansworth	5 59	6 40	6 54	....	7 23	....	7 39	....	7 48	....	7 59	....	8 13	....	8 21	....	8 28	....	8 40	....	8 51	....
Moor Pk. & Sandy Lodge	..	6 44	7 2	7 5	7 31	7 34	7 47	7 50	7 56	7 59	8 7	8 10	8 18	..	..	8 30	8 36	8 40	8 45	8 51	8 58	9 1
Northwood	6 7	6 47	....	7 8	....	7 37	....	7 53	....	8 2	....	8 13	8 22	....	8 29	8 33	....	8 43	8 50	8 54	....	9 4
Pinner	6 14	6 53	..	7 14	..	7 43	..	7 59	..	8 8	..	8 19	8 27	..	..	8 39	..	8 49	..	8 59	..	9 9
Harrow-on-the-Hill	6 22	7 1	....	7 23	....	7 50	....	8 7	....	8 15	....	8 26	8 34	....	8 43	8 46	....	8 57	9 1	9 6	....	9 16
Baker Street	..	7 22	7 29	7 43	8 2	8 10	8 17	8 29	8 26	8 33	8 36	8 45	¶	..	..	9 6	9 9	9 18	..	9 25	9 28	9 35
Marylebone	6 37	‡	‡	....	‡	‡	‡	‡	....	....	‡	....	8 50	....	8 58	‡	‡	‡	9 18	‡	‡	‡

No. 2.																			
AYLESBURY	8 17	....	8 41	....	....	9 15	....	9 44	9 56	....	10 40	....	11 25	....	12 10	....	1 5	....	1 10
STOKE MAND'VILLE	8 24	..	8 48	..	..	9 22	..	..	10 3	..	10 47	..	11 32	..	12 17	..	..	..	1 17
WENDOVER	8 31	....	8 55	....	....	9 29	....	....	10 10	....	10 54	....	11 39	....	12 24	....		....	1 24
Great Missenden	8 41	..	9 5	9 13	..	9 39	..	..	10 20	..	11 4	..	11 49	..	12 34	..	Restaurant Car	..	1 34
Amersham	8 51	....	9 15	9 23	....	9 49	....	A10 11	10 30	....	11 15	....	11 59	....	12 44	....		....	1 44
Chesham dep.	8 45	..	..	9 17	..	9 43	..	..	10 24	..	11 9	..	11 53	..	12 38	..		1 13	1 38
Chalfont & Latimer	8 56	....	....	9 28	....	9 54	....	....	10 35	....	11 20	....	12 4	....	12 49	....		1 22	1 49
Chorley Wood	9 0	..	..	9 32	..	9 58	..	..	10 39	..	11 24	..	12 8	..	12 53	..		..	1 53
Rickmansworth	9 5	....	....	9 37	....	10 3	....	....	10 44	....	11 29	....	12 13	....	12 58	....		....	1 58
Moor Pk. & Sandy Lodge	9 13	9 18	..	9 42	9 45	10 10	10 13	..	10 51	10 57	11 34	11 40	12 21	12 25	1 6	1 10		..	2 6
Northwood	....	9 21	....	....	9 48	....	10 16	....	....	11 0	11 38	11 43	....	12 28	....	1 13		....	....
Pinner	..	9 26	..	..	9 53	..	10 21	..	..	11 5	..	11 48	..	12 33	..	1 18		..	..
Harrow-on-the-Hill	....	9 32	....	9 54	9 59	....	10 27	10 35	11 2	11 11	11 49	11 55	12 32	12 40	1 17	1 25	....	....	2 17
Baker Street	9 40	9 52	¶	..	10 19	10 37	10 47	¶	11 20	11 31	..	12 16	12 50	1 1	1 35	1 46	¶	..	2 35
Marylebone	‡	‡	9 51	10 11	....	....	....	10 50	....	..	12 8	....	....	....	....	....	1 58	....	....

‡–Through train to City. ¶–First and third class. A–Arr. 4 minutes earlier.

55

A timetable produced by London Transport in 1950 shows the service provided by them until 1960 a through service of trains operated between Aylesbury and Liverpool Street.

AYLESBURY - AMERSHAM - HARROW - LONDON — **Metropolitan Line Table 1**

All trains third class only except where otherwise stated.

MONDAY TO FRIDAY–contd.

No. 3.																					
AYLESBURY	....	1 41	2 7	....	2 54	....	3 35	3 40	4 5	....	4 33	....	....	4 48	5 18	....	....	5 46	....	6 23	....
STOKE MAND'VILLE	..	1 48	2 14	..	3 1	..	..	3 47	4 12	..	4 40	..	..	4 55	5 25	..	..	5 53	..	6 30	..
WENDOVER	....	1 55	2 21	....	3 8	....		3 54	4 19	....	4 47	....	....	5 3	5 32	....	....	6 0	....	6 37	....
Great Missenden	..	2 5	2 31	..	3 18	..		4 4	4 29	..	4 57	..	..	5 14	5 42	..	..	6 10	..	6 47	..
Amersham	....	2 15	2 41	....	3 28	....	Restaurant Car	4 15	4 39	....	5 7	....	....	5 25	5 52	....	....	6 20	....	6 57	....
Chesham dep.	..	2 9	2 35	..	3 22	..		4 3	4 34	..	5 1	..	..	..	5 41	..	..	6 14	..	..	..
Chalfont & Latimer	....	2 20	2 46	....	3 33	....		4 20	4 45	....	5 12	....	....	5 30	5 57	....	....	6 25	....	7 2	....
Chorley Wood	..	2 24	2 50	..	3 37	..		4 24	4 49	..	5 16	..	..	5 37	6 1	..	..	6 29	..	7 6	..
Rickmansworth	....	2 29	2 55	....	3 42	....		4 29	4 54	....	5 21	....	....	5 42	6 6	....	....	6 34	....	7 11	....
Moor Pk. & Sandy Lodge	2 10	..	3 2	3 10	3 50	3 55		4 34	5 2	5 8	5 29	5 33	..	5 47	6 13	6 16	..	6 42	6 45	7 19	7 22
Northwood	2 13	2 37	....	3 13	....	3 58		4 38	....	5 11	....	5 36	....	5 51	....	6 19	....	....	6 48	....	7 25
Pinner	2 18	2 42	..	3 18	..	4 3	..	4 43	..	5 16	..	5 41	.	5 56	..	6 25	..	..	6 54	..	7 31
Harrow-on-the-Hill	2 25	2 49	3 13	3 24	4 1	4 9	....	4 50	5 15	5 23	5 40	5 47	....	6 4	6 26	6 31	....	6 55	7 0	7 32	7 37
Baker Street	2 46	..	3 32	3 44	4 20	4 29	¶	..	5 35	5 44	6 0	6 7	..	¶	6 46	6 51	..	*7 19	..	7 52	7 58
Marylebone	....	3 7	‡	‡	‡	‡	4 28	5 11	‡	‡	‡	....	....	6 19	....	....	....	....	....	....	....

No. 4.																			
AYLESBURY	....	....	6 48	....	7 10	7 33	....	7 54	8 35	8 40	....	9 10	....	9 37	10 14	....	10 59	....	....
STOKE MAND'VILLE	..	..	6 55	..	7 17	7 40	..	8 1		8 47	..	9 17	..	9 44	10 21	..	11 6	..	..
WENDOVER	....	....	7 2	....	7 24	7 47	....	8 9		8 54	....	9 24	....	9 51	10 28	....	11 13	....	....
Great Missenden	..	..	7 12	..	7 34	7 57	..	8 20		9 4	..	9 34	..	10 1	10 38	..	11 23	..	..
Amersham	....	....	7 22	....	7 46	8 7	....	8 31		9 14	....	9 44	....	10 11	10 48	....	11 33	....	....
Chesham dep.	7 2	..	..	..	7 28	7 58	..	8 25	Restaurant Car	9 5	..	9 38	..	..	10 42	..	11 27	..	12 40
Chalfont & Latimer	7 12	....	7 27	....	7 51	8 12	....	8 36		9 19	....	9 49	....	10 16	10 53	....	11 38	....	12 49
Chorley Wood	7 16	..	7 31	..	7 55	8 16	..	8 40		9 23	..	9 53	..	10 20	10 57	..	11 42	..	..
Rickmansworth	7 21	....	7 36	....	8 0	8 21	....	8 45		9 28	....	9 58	....	10 25	11 2	....	11 47	....	....
Moor Pk. & Sandy Lodge	7 29	7 35	7 44	7 50	8 8	8 28	8 36	8 52		9 35	9 38	10 5	10 8	10 30	11 9	11 12	11 54	11 57	..
Northwood	....	7 38	....	7 53	8 12	....	8 39	8 56		....	9 41	....	10 11	10 34	....	11 15	....	12 0	....
Pinner	..	7 44	..	7 59	8 19	.	8 44	9 3	..	..	9 46	..	10 16	10 41	..	11 20	..	12 6	..
Harrow-on-the-Hill	7 41	7 51	7 55	8 6	8 28	8 39	8 51	9 13	9 20	9 47	9 52	10 17	10 23	10 49	11 19	11 26	12 5	12 13	..
Baker Street	*8 4	8 12	*8 19	8 27	..	8 58	9 12	..	¶	*10 7	10 13	10 37	10 43	..	11 39	..	*12 29	..	..
Marylebone	....	....	....	....	8 43	....	....	9 28	9 34	....	....	....	....	11 7	....	....	....	....	....

¶–First and third class. ‡–Through train to City *–Change at Wembley Park.

57

Particularly interesting is the twice daily Restaurant Car service to Marylebone.

AYLESBURY - AMERSHAM - HARROW - LONDON — **Metropolitan Line Table 1**

SATURDAY — All trains third class only except where otherwise stated

No. 5.																					
AYLESBURY	....	....	6 6	....	....	6 35	....	....	6 51	....	....	....	....	....	7 11	....	7 25	....	7 38	....	....
STOKE MAND'VILLE	..	..	6 13	..	..	6 42	..	..	6 58	..	..	..	..	..	7 18	..	7 32	..	..	..	..
WENDOVER	....	....	6 20	....	....	6 49	....	....	7 5	....	....	....	....	....	7 25	....	7 39	....	7 50	....	....
Great Missenden	..	..	6 30	..	..	6 59	..	..	7 15	..	..	..	..	..	7 35	..	7 49	..	..	..	..
Amersham	....	....	6 40	....	....	7 9	....	....	7 25	....	....	....	....	....	7 45	....	8 0	....	8 7	....	....
Chesham dep.	5 41	..	6 34	..	..	7 3	..	..	..	..	..	7 29	..	..	..	..	7 54	..	..	..	8 9
Chalfont & Latimer	5 5C	....	6 45	....	....	7 14	....	....	7 30	....	....	7 39	....	....	7 50	....	8 5	....	8 12	....	8 19
Chorley Wood	5 54	..	6 49	..	..	7 18	..	..	7 34	..	..	7 43	..	..	7 54	..	..	..	8 16	..	8 23
Rickmansworth	5 59	6 40	6 54	....	....	7 23	....	....	7 39	....	....	7 48	....	....	7 59	....	8 13	....	8 21	....	8 28
MoorPk.& Sandy Lodge	..	6 44	7 1	..	7 4	7 31	..	7 34	7 47	..	7 50	7 56	7 59	..	8 7	8 10	8 18	..	..	8 31	8 36
Northwood	6 7	6 47	....	....	7 7	....	....	7 37	....	....	7 53	....	8 2	....	....	8 13	8 22	....	8 29	8 34	....
Pinner	6 14	6 53	..	..	7 13	..	..	7 43	..	..	7 59	..	8 8	..	..	8 19	8 27	..	..	8 40	..
Harrow-on-the-Hill	6 22	7 1	....	....	7 20	....	....	7 51	....	....	8 7	....	8 15	....	....	8 26	8 34	...	8 43	8 48	....
Baker Street	..	7 22	7 29	..	7 40	8 2	..	8 11	8 18	..	8 29	8 27	8 34	..	8 36	8 45	¶	..	..	9 10	9 7
Marylebone	6 37	‡	‡	....	‡	‡	....	‡	‡	....	‡	....	....	....	‡	‡	8 50	....	8 58	‡	‡

No. 6.																			
AYLESBURY	....	7 51	....	8 3	....	8 17	....	....	8 41	....	....	....	9 15	....	9 44	9 54	....	10 40	....
STOKE MAND'VILLE	..	7 58	..	8 10	..	8 24	..	..	8 48	..	..	..	9 22	..	..	10 1	..	10 47	..
WENDOVER	....	8 5	....	8 17	....	8 31	....	....	8 55	....	....	....	9 29	....	....	10 8	....	10 54	....
Great Missenden	..	8 15	..	8 27	..	8 41	..	..	9 5	9 13	..	..	9 39	..	..	10 18	..	11 4	..
Amersham	....	8 25	....	8 37	....	8 51	....	....	9 15	9 23	....	....	9 49	....	A10 11	10 28	....	11 15	....
Chesham dep.	..	..	..	..	..	8 45	..	..	..	9 17	..	..	9 43	..	..	10 22	..	11 9	..
Chalfont & Latimer	....	8 31	....	8 42	....	8 56	....	....	....	9 28	....	....	9 54	....	....	10 33	....	11 20	....
Chorley Wood	..	8 35	..	8 46	..	9 0	..	..	..	9 32	..	..	9 58	..	..	10 37	..	11 24	..
Rickmansworth	....	8 40	....	8 51	....	9 5	....	....	....	9 37	....	....	10 3	....	....	10 42	....	11 29	....
MoorPk.& Sandy Lodge	8 39	8 45	8 50	8 58	9 1	9 13	..	9 17	..	9 42	9 45	¶	10 10	10 13	..	10 49	10 57	11 34	11 40
Northwood	8 42	8 50	8 53	....	9 4	....	....	9 20	....	....	9 48	....	....	10 16	....	....	11 0	11 38	11 43
Pinner	8 48	..	8 58	..	9 9	..	..	9 25	..	..	9 53	..	..	10 21	..	..	11 5	..	11 48
Harrow-on-the-Hill	8 56	9 1	9 5	....	9 15	....	....	9 31	....	9 54	9 59	....	....	10 27	10 35	11 0	11 11	11 49	11 54
Baker Street	9 16	..	9 24	9 29	9 34	9 40	..	9 52	¶	..	10 20	..	10 37	10 47	¶	11 19	11 31	..	12 14
Marylebone	‡	9 18	‡	‡	....	‡	....	‡	9 51	10 11	‡	....	....	....	10 50	‡	..	12 8	‡

‡–Through train to City. ¶–First and third class. A–Arrives 4 minutes earlier.

59

AYLESBURY - AMERSHAM - HARROW - LONDON **Metropolitan Line Table 1**

All trains third class only except where otherwise stated.

SATURDAY–continued

No. 7.																					
AYLESBURY	11 25	....	12 3	....	12 35	1 5	....	1 10	....	....	1 41	2 5	....	2 31	2 36	....	....	3 1	3 35	....	3 40
STOKE MAND'VILLE	11 32	..	12 10	..	12 42	..	..	1 17	..	..	1 48	2 12	..		2 43	..	..	3 8	..	..	3 47
WENDOVER	11 39	....	12 17	....	12 49		....	1 24	....	1 40	1 55	2 19	....		2 50	....	....	3 15		....	3 54
Great Missenden	11 49	..	12 27	..	12 59		..	1 34	..	1 50	2 5	2 29	..		3 0	..	..	3 25		..	4 4
Amersham	11 59	....	12 37	....	1 9		....	1 44	....	2 0	2 15	2 39	....		3 10	....	----	3 35		....	4 15
Chesham .... dep.	11 53	..	12 31	..	1 3	Restaurant Car	..	..	..	1 54	..	2 33	..	Restaurant Car	..	..	..	3 26	Restaurant Car	..	4 3
Chalfont & Latimer	12 4	....	12 42	....	1 14		....	1 49	....	2 5	2 20	2 45	....		3 15	....	....	3 41		....	4 20
Chorley Wood	12 8	..	12 46	..	1 18		..	1 53	..	2 9	2 24	2 49	..		3 19	..	..	3 45		..	4 24
Rickmansworth	12 13	....	12 51	....	1 23		....	1 58	....	2 14	2 29	2 54	....		3 24	....	....	3 50		....	4 29
Moor Pk. & Sandy Lodge	12 21	12 24	12 59	1 2	1 30		1 38	2 7	2 11	2 19	..	3 2	3 9		3 32	3 36	..	3 58		4 8	4 34
Northwood	....	12 27	....	1 5	....		1 41	....	2 14	2 23	2 37	....	3 12		....	3 39	....	....		4 11	4 38
Pinner	..	12 32	..	1 11	..		1 47	..	2 20	2 28	2 42	..	3 17	..	..	3 44	..	..		4 16	4 43
Harrow-on-the-Hill	12 35	12 38	1 11	1 17	1 41	....	1 53	2 19	2 26	2 35	2 49	3 15	3 23	....	3 43	3 51	....	4 9	....	4 22	4 54
Baker Street	12 55	12 59	1 32	1 37	2 0	¶	2 14	2 39	2 46	..	..	3 35	3 43	¶	*4 5	4 12	..	4 28	¶	4 42	..
Marylebone	‡	....	‡	....	‡	1 58	....	‡	....	2 50	3 7	....	....	3 29	....	....	....	....	4 28	....	5 11

No. 8.																						
AYLESBURY	4 3	....	4 31	....	4 48	....	5 15	5 47	....	6 18	....	6 47	7 20	....	8 2	....	8 35	8 45	....	9 28	....	....
STOKE MAND'VILLE	4 10	..	4 38	..	4 55	..	5 22	5 54	..	6 25	..	6 54	7 27	..	8 9	..	..	8 52	..	9 35	..	..
WENDOVER	4 17	....	4 45	....	5 3	....	5 30	6 1	....	6 32	....	7 1	7 34	....	8 16	....		8 59	....	9 42	....	....
Great Missenden	4 27	..	4 55	..	5 14	..	5 40	6 11	..	6 42	..	7 11	7 44	..	8 26	..		9 9	..	9 52	..	..
Amersham	4 37	....	5 5	....	5 25	....	5 51	6 21	..	6 52	....	7 22	7 54	....	8 36	....		9 19	....	10 2	....	....
Chesham .... dep.	4 31	..	4 59	..	..	..	5 47	6 15	..	6 46	..	7 16	7 48	..	8 30	..	Restaurant Car	9 14	..	9 49	..	10 18
Chalfont & Latimer	4 42	....	5 10	....	5 30	....	5 58	6 26	....	6 57	....	7 27	7 59	....	8 41	....		9 25	....	10 8	....	10 27
Chorley Wood	4 46	..	5 14	..	5 37	..	6 2	6 30	..	7 1	..	7 31	8 3	..	8 45	..		9 29	..	10 12	..	..
Rickmansworth	4 51	....	5 19	....	5 42	....	6 7	6 35	....	7 6	....	7 36	8 8	....	8 50	....		9 34	9 47	10 17	....	....
Moor Pk. & Sandy Lodge	4 59	5 6	5 27	5 36	5 47	..	6 12	6 43	6 51	7 14	7 21	7 41	8 16	8 21	8 58	9 2		9 42	9 51	10 25	10 37	..
Northwood	....	5 9	....	5 39	5 51	....	6 16	....	6 54	....	7 24	7 45	....	8 24	....	9 5		....	9 54	....	10 40	....
Pinner	..	5 14	..	5 44	5 56	..	6 23	..	6 59	..	7 29	7 52	..	8 29	..	9 10	..	..	9 59	..	10 45	..
Harrow-on-the-Hill	5 10	5 21	5 38	5 50	6 4	....	6 31	6 54	7 5	7 25	7 35	8 0	8 27	8 35	9 9	9 18	9 20	9 53	10 5	10 36	10 52	....
Baker Street	5 29	5 42	5 57	6 11	¶	..	..	7 14	7 26	7 44	7 56	..	8 46	8 56	9 28	9 38	¶	10 13	10 26	*10 56	11 12	..
Marylebone	....	....	....	....	6 19	....	6 46	....		....	....	8 15	....	....	....	....	9 34	....	....	..	....	....

‡–Through train to City. ¶–First and third class. *–Change at Wembley Park.

AYLESBURY - AMERSHAM - HARROW - LONDON **Metropolitan Line Table 1**

All trains third class only except where otherwise stated.

No. 9.	SATURDAY–continued								SUNDAY									
AYLESBURY	10 14	....	10 59	....	....	....	....	....	....	....	8 0	8 45	9 30	10 12	11 0	11 45	12 30	1 15
STOKE MAND'VILLE	10 21	..	11 6	..	..	..	..	..	..	..	8 6	8 51	9 36	10 18	11 6	11 51	12 36	1 21
WENDOVER	10 28	....	11 13	....	....	....	....	....	....	....	8 13	8 58	9 43	10 26	11 13	11 58	12 43	1 28
Great Missenden	10 38	..	11 23	..	..	..	..	..	..	..	8 23	9 8	9 53	10 37	11 23	12 8	12 53	1 38
Amersham	10 48	....	11 33	....	....	....	....	....	....	....	8 33	9 18	10 3	10 48	11 33	12 18	1 3	1 48
Chesham .... dep.	10 42	..	11 27	..	12 40	..	..	..	7 25	..	8 28	9 5	9 56	10 43	11 27	12 12	12 57	1 42
Chalfont & Latimer	10 53	....	11 38	....	12 49	....	....	....	7 34	....	8 38	9 23	10 8	10 54	11 38	12 23	1 8	1 53
Chorley Wood	10 57	..	11 42	..	..	..	..	..	7 38	..	8 42	9 27	10 12	10 58	11 42	12 27	1 12	1 57
Rickmansworth	11 2	....	11 47	....	....	....	....	....	7 43	....	8 47	9 32	10 17	11 3	11 47	12 32	1 17	2 2
Moor Pk. & Sandy Lodge	11 9	11 12	11 54	11 57	..	..	..	..	7 51	7 54	8 54	9 39	10 24	11 9	11 54	12 39	1 24	2 9
Northwood	....	11 15	....	12 0	....	....	....	....	....	7 57	8 57	9 42	10 27	11 14	11 57	12 42	1 27	2 12
Pinner	..	11 20	..	12 6	..	..	..	..	..	8 3	9 3	9 48	10 33	11 21	12 3	12 48	1 33	2 18
Harrow-on-the-Hill	11 19	11 26	12 5	12 13	....	....	....	....	8 2	8 9	9 11	9 55	10 40	11 30	12 10	12 56	1 40	2 26
Baker Street	11 39	..	*12 29	..	..	..	..	..	*8 22	8 30	9 30	10 15	11 0	¶	12 30	1 15	2 0	2 45
Marylebone	....	....	....	....	....	....	....	....	....	....	....	....	....	11 45	....	....	....	....

SUNDAY–continued

No. 10.																						
AYLESBURY	2 0	2 45	3 24	3 30	....	4 15	4 45	....	5 24	....	5 54	....	6 27	....	7 5	....	7 38	....	....	8 13	8 20	....
STOKE MAND'VILLE	2 6	2 51		3 36	..	4 21	4 51	..	5 30	..	6 0	..	6 33	..	7 11	..	7 44	..	..	..	8 26	..
WENDOVER	2 13	2 58		3 43	....	4 29	4 58	....	5 37	....	6 7	....	6 40	....	7 18	....	7 51	....	....	....	8 33	....
Great Missenden	2 23	3 8		3 53	..	4 40	5 8	..	5 47	..	6 17	..	6 50	..	7 28	..	8 1	..	..	..	8 43	..
Amersham	2 33	3 18		4 3	....	4 51	5 18	....	5 57	....	6 27	....	7 0	....	7 38	....	8 11	....	....	....	8 53	....
Chesham .... dep.	2 27	3 12	Restaurant Car	..	..	4 43	5 12	..	5 50	..	6 14	..	6 54	..	7 26	..	8 5	..	..	..	8 47	..
Chalfont & Latimer	2 38	3 23		4 8	....	4 57	5 23	....	6 2	....	6 32	....	7 5	....	7 43	....	8 16	....	....	....	8 58	....
Chorley Wood	2 42	3 27		4 12	..	5 1	5 27	..	6 6	..	6 36	..	7 9	..	7 47	..	8 20	..	..	..	9 2	..
Rickmansworth	2 47	3 32		4 17	....	5 6	5 32	....	6 11	....	6 41	....	7 14	....	7 52	....	8 25	....	....	....	9 7	9 20
Moor Pk. & Sandy Lodge	2 54	3 39		4 24	..	5 12	5 39	..	6 20	..	6 48	6 54	7 21	7 24	8 0	8 9	8 32	8 39	..	..	9 15	9 24
Northwood	2 57	3 42	....	4 27	....	5 17	5 42	....	6 23	....	....	6 57	....	7 27	....	8 12	....	8 42	....	....	....	9 27
Pinner	3 3	3 48	..	4 33	..	5 24	5 48	..	6 29	..	..	7 2	..	7 32	..	8 17	..	8 47	..	..	..	9 32
Harrow-on-the-Hill	3 10	3 56	4 13	4 41	....	5 33	5 56	....	6 37	....	6 58	7 8	7 34	7 38	8 12	8 23	8 43	8 53	....	9 2	9 27	9 38
Baker Street	3 30	4 15	¶	5 0	..	..	6 15	..	6 56	..	7 18	7 29	7 54	7 59	8 32	8 44	9 3	9 14	..	¶	9 47	9 59
Marylebone	....	....	4 30	....	....	5 48	....	....	....	....	....	....	....	....	....	....	....	....	....	9 20	....	....

* Change at Wembley Park. ¶–First and third class.

AYLESBURY - AMERSHAM - HARROW - LONDON **Metropolitan Line Table 1**

All trains third class only except where otherwise stated.

SUNDAY–continued

No. 11												
AYLESBURY	8 45	8 51	....	9 23	....	....	10 5	....	....	....	----	....
STOKE MANDEVILLE		8 57	..	9 29	..	..	10 11	..	..	..	..	..
WENDOVER		9 4	....	9 36	....	....	10 18	....	....	....	----	....
Great Missenden		9 14	..	9 46	..	..	10 28	..	..	..	..	..
Amersham		9 24	....	9 56	....	----	10 38	....	....	....	----	....
Chesham .... dep.	Restaurant Car	..	..	9 46	..	..	10 26	..	10 56	11 41	..	..
Chalfont & Latimer		9 29	....	10 1	....	....	10 43	....	11 5	11 50	----	....
Chorley Wood		9 33	..	10 5	..	..	10 47	..	..	..	..	..
Rickmansworth		9 38	....	10 10	....	....	10 52	....	....	....	....	....
Moor Park & Sandy Lodge		9 46	9 54	10 18	10 25	..	11 0	11 13	..	..	..	..
Northwood	....	....	9 57	....	10 28	....	....	11 16	....	....	----	....
Pinner	..	..	10 2	..	10 33	..		11 21	..	..	..	..
Harrow on the Hill	9 31	9 57	10 8	10 28	10 40	....	11 12	11 27	....	....	----	....
Baker Street	¶	10 17	10 29	*10 51	11 2	..	11 31	11 52	..	..	..	..
Marylebone	9 50	....	....	....	....	....	....	....	....	....	....	....

A–Arrives 4 minutes earlier.
*–Change at Wembley Park.
‡–Through train from City.
§–Sets down only.
¶–First and third class.

MONDAY to FRIDAY

No. 1.																				
Marylebone	3 45	....	....	5 50	....	....	....	....	....	....	7 22	....	....	7 45	....	‡	....	8 37	‡	‡
Baker Street	¶	*5 10	5 45	..	..	..	6 33	..	7 5	7 12	..	..	..	¶	7 54	8 8	..	..	9 4	9 16
Harrow-on-the-Hill	....	5 37	6 6	6 20	....	6 48	6 55	....	7 27	7 34	7 40	....	8 3	8 7	8 16	8 27	....	8 56	9 28	9 36
Pinner	..	5 43	6 12	6 28	..	6 53	..	..	7 32	..	7 47	..	8 8	..	8 21	..	..	9 2	9 33	..
Northwood	....	5 50	6 19	6 36	....	6 59	....	....	7 38	....	7 56	....	8 14	8 18	8 27	....	....	9 8	9 39	....
Moor Pk. & Sandy Lodge	..	..	..	6 39	..	7 2	7 5	..	7 41	7 44	7 59	..	8 17	8 21	8 30	8 37	..	9 11	9 42	9 46
Rickmansworth	....	6 0	6 30	6 45	....	....	7 13	....	....	7 52	8 4	....	....	8 28	....	8 45	....	9 16	....	9 53
Chorley Wood	..	6 8	6 38	6 53	..	..	7 21	..	..	8 0	8 12	..	..	8 35	..	8 53	..	9 24	..	10 1
Chalfont & Latimer	....	6 16	6 45	7 0	....	....	7 28	....	....	8 7	8 19	....	....	8 42	....	9 0	....	9 31	....	10 8
Chesham .... arr.	..	6 25	6 56	..	..	..	7 50	..	..	..	8 30	..	..	..	..	9 11	..	9 41	..	10 19
Amersham	....	....	6 52	7 7	....	....	7 35	....	....	8 14	8 26	....	....	8 51	....	9 7	....	9 38	....	10 15
Great Missenden	..	..	7 1	7 16	..	..	7 44	..	..	8 23	8 35	..	..	9 1	..	9 16	..	9 47	..	10 24
WENDOVER	§5 0	....	7 10	7 25	....	....	7 53	....	....	8 32	....	....	....	A9 13	....	9 25	....	9 56	....	10 33
STOKE MAND'VILLE	..	..	7 15	....	..	..	7 58	..	..	8 37	..	..	..	..	..	9 30	..	10 1	..	10 38
AYLESBURY	5 12	....	7 20	7 33	....	....	8 3	....	....	8 42	....	....	....	9 21	....	9 35	....	10 6	....	10 43

LONDON - HARROW - AMERSHAM - AYLESBURY Metropolitan Line Table 1

All trains third class only except where otherwise stated.

MONDAY to FRIDAY–continued

No. 2.																			
Marylebone	....	10 0	‡	10 15	....	....	....	....	12 25	....	....	....	1 25	....	....	....	....	....	3 20
Baker Street	9 49	¶	10 5	..	11 6	11 15	11 51	12 0	..	12 51	1 0	..	¶	1 51	2 0	2 35	2 45	3 6	¶
Harrow-on-the-Hill	10 11	10 19	10 23	10 34	11 27	11 34	12 12	12 19	12 44	1 12	1 19	....	1 44	2 12	2 19	2 56	3 3	3 27	3 39
Pinner	10 16	..	..	10 41	11 32	..	12 17	..	12 51	1 17	..	..	1 50	2 17	..	3 1	..	3 32	..
Northwood	10 22		....	10 50	11 38	....	12 23	....	1 0	1 23	....	....	1 57	2 23	....	3 7	....	3 38	....
Moor Pk. & Sandy Lodge	10 25	Restaurant Car	10 33	10 53	11 41	11 44	12 26	12 29	1 3	1 26	1 29	..	2 0	2 26	2 29	3 10	3 13	3 41	Restaurant Car
Rickmansworth	....		10 40	10 59	....	11 52	....	12 37	1 9	....	1 37	....	2 6	....	2 37	....	3 21	....	
Chorley Wood	..		10 48	11 7	..	12 0	..	12 45	1 17	..	1 45	..	2 14	..	2 45	..	3 29	..	
Chalfont & Latimer	....		10 55	11 15	....	12 7	....	12 52	1 25	....	1 52	....	2 22	....	2 52	....	3 36	....	
Chesham .... arr.	..		11 6	11 30	..	12 18	..	1 3	1 35	..	2 3	..	2 32	..	3 3	..	3 47	..	
Amersham	....		11 2	11 22	....	12 14	....	12 59	1 32	....	1 59	....	2 29	....	2 59	....	3 43	....	
Great Missenden	..		11 11	11 31	..	12 23	..	1 8	1 41	..	2 8	..	2 38	..	3 8	..	3 52	..	
WENDOVER	....		11 20	11 40	....	12 32	....	1 17	1 50	....	2 17	....	2 47	....	3 17	....	4 1	....	..
STOKE MAND'VILLE	..		11 25	11 45	..	12 37	..	1 22	1 55	..	2 22	..	2 52	..	3 22	..	4 6	..	....
AYLESBURY	....	11 0	11 30	11 50	....	12 42	....	1 27	2 0	....	2 27	....	2 57	....	3 27	....	4 11	....	4 20

No. 3.																						
Marylebone	....	....	‡	‡	‡	‡	4 50	5 0	‡	....	5 7	5 22	‡	‡	..	‡	‡	‡	‡	6 8	‡	‡
Baker Street	3 23	3 46	3 58	4 12	4 26	4 45	¶	¶	5 1	4 59	..	....	5 22	5 31	5 29	5 41	5 46	5 56	6 1	¶	6 8	6 16
Harrow-on-the-Hill	....	4 8	....	4 35	....	5 7	....	....	....	5 21	5 25	5 40	5 43	..	5 52	....	6 5	....	6 20	....	6 28	....
Pinner	..	4 13	..	4 40	..	5 12		..	..	5 26	..	5 46	5 49	....	5 58	..	6 11	..	6 26	6 30	6 34	..
Northwood	....	4 19	....	4 46	....	5 18		....	....	5 32	5 38	5 52	5 55	..	6 4	....	6 18	....	6 33	6 36	6 41	....
Moor Pk. & Sandy Lodge	3 51	4 22	4 25	4 49	4 53	5 21	Restaurant Car	..	5 29	5 35	5 41	5 55	5 58	6 2	6 7	6 12	6 21	6 24	6 36	6 39	6 44	6 47
Rickmansworth	3 59	....	4 32	....	5 0	....		....	5 37	....	5 47	6 0	..	6 10	..	6 20	....	6 32	....	6 44	....	6 55
Chorley Wood	4 7	..	4 40	..	5 8	..		..	5 45	..	5 55	6 8	....	6 18	....	6 28	..	6 40	..	..	..	7 3
Chalfont & Latimer	4 14	....	4 47	....	5 15	....		....	5 52	....	6 2	6 15	..	6 26	..	6 35	....	6 47	....	....	....	7 10
Chesham .... arr.	4 25	..	4 58	..	5 26	..		..	6 8	..	..	....	....	6 35	....	..	..	6 56	..	..	..	7 21
Amersham	4 21	....	4 54	..	5 22	....		5 45	5 59	....	6 9	6 22	..	..	..	6 42	....	....	....	7 2	....	7 17
Great Missenden	4 30	..	5 3	..	A5 42	..		5 54	6 8	..	6 18	6 31	....	....	....	6 51	..	..	..	7 11	..	7 26
WENDOVER	4 39	....	5 12	....	5 51	....		6 3	6 17	....	6 27	6 40	..	..	..	7 0	....	....	....	7 20	....	7 35
STOKE MAND'VILLE	4 44	..	5 17	..	5 56	..	..	6 8	6 22	..	6 32	6 45	....	....	....	7 5	..	..	..	7 25	..	7 40
AYLESBURY	4 49	....	5 22	....	6 1	....	5 48	6 13	6 27	....	6 37	6 50	..	..	..	7 10	....	....	....	7 30	....	7 45

‡–Through train from City. ¶–First and third class. A–Arrives 5 30 p.m.

The Met had ten horseboxes that were regularly used in the Chilterns this is no 10 Wendover van in the siding at Wendover yard. It was built by G R Turner and was scrapped in 1938.

H C Casserley

LONDON - HARROW - AMERSHAM - AYLESBURY **Metropolitan Line Table 1**

All trains third class only except where otherwise stated.

No. 4. MONDAY to FRIDAY–continued

Marylebone	6 26	‡	‡	....	....	....	....	7 45	....	....	....	....	10 0	....	....	....	....	....	....	....
Baker Street	..	6 38	6 47	7 2	7 17	..	7 37	..	8 5	8 23	8 50	9 8	¶	9 52	10 8	10 50	11 0	11 51	12 0	..
Harrow-on-the-Hill	6 44	6 58	....	7 26	....	....	7 59	8 7	8 29	8 42	9 14	9 27	....	10 16	10 27	11 14	11 22	12 14	12 22	....
Pinner	6 51	7 4	..	7 32	..	..	8 5	8 15	8 34	..	9 19	..	..	10 21	..	11 19	..	12 19	..	..
Northwood	6 57	7 10	....	7 38	....	....	8 11	8 23	8 40	....	9 25	....	....	10 27	....	11 25	....	12 25	....	....
Moor Pk. & Sandy Lodge	7 0	7 13	7 16	7 41	7 45	..	8 14	8 26	8 43	8 52	9 28	9 37	..	10 30	10 37	11 28	11 32	12 28	12 32	..
Rickmansworth	7 5	....	7 24	....	7 53	....	....	8 32	....	9 0	....	9 45	....	....	10 45	....	11 40	....	12 40	....
Chorley Wood	7 13	..	7 32	..	8 1	..	..	8 40	..	9 8	..	9 53	..	..	10 53	..	11 48	..	12 48	..
Chalfont & Latimer	7 20	....	7 39	....	8 9	....	....	8 47	....	9 16	....	10 0	....	....	11 0	....	11 55	....	12 55	....
Chesham arr.	..	..	7 50	..	8 21	..	..	8 58	..	9 28	..	10 11	..	..	11 11	..	12 6	..	1 6	..
Amersham	7 28	....	7 46	....	8 16	....	....	8 55	....	9 23	..	10 7	....	....	11 7	....	12 2	....	1 2	....
Great Missenden	7 37	..	7 55	..	8 25	..	..	9 4	..	9 32	..	10 16	..	..	11 16	..	12 11	..	1 11	..
WENDOVER	7 46	....	8 4	....	8 34	....	....	9 13	....	9 41	....	10 25	....	....	11 25	....	12 20	....	1 20	....
STOKE MAND'VILLE	7 51	..	8 9	..	8 39	..	..	9 18	..	9 46	..	10 30	..	..	11 30	..	12 25	..	1 25	..
AYLESBURY	7 56	....	8 14	....	8 44	....	....	9 23	....	9 51	....	10 35	10 55	....	11 35	....	12 30	....	1 30	....

No. 5. SATURDAY

Marylebone	3 45	....	....	5 50	....	..	....	....	....	....	7 22	....	7 45	....	‡	8 37	‡	‡
Baker Street	¶	*5 10	5 45	..	..	....	6 33	7 5	7 12	..	..	..	¶	7 54	8 8	..	9 2	9 16
Harrow-on-the-Hill	....	5 37	6 6	6 20	....	6 48	6 55	7 27	7 34	....	7 40	8 1	8 7	8 15	8 27	8 56	9 27	9 36
Pinner	..	5 43	6 12	6 28	..	6 53	..	7 32	..	..	7 47	8 6	..	8 20	..	9 2	9 32	..
Northwood	....	5 50	6 19	6 36	....	6 59	..	7 38	..	....	7 56	8 12	8 18	8 26	..	9 8	9 38	....
Moor Pk. & Sandy Lodge	..	..	..	6 39	..	7 2	7 5	7 41	7 44	..	7 59	8 15	8 21	8 29	8 37	9 11	9 41	9 46
Rickmansworth	....	6 0	6 30	6 45	....	..	7 13	..	7 52	....	8 4	....	8 28	....	8 45	9 16	....	9 53
Chorley Wood	..	6 8	6 38	6 53	..	....	7 21	....	8 0	..	8 12	..	8 35	..	8 53	9 24	..	10 1
Chalfont & Latimer	....	6 16	6 45	7 0	....	..	7 28	..	8 7	....	8 19	....	8 42	....	9 0	9 31	....	10 8
Chesham arr.	..	6 25	6 56	..	..	....	7 50	....	..	..	8 30	..	..	..	9 11	9 41	..	10 19
Amersham	....	....	6 52	7 7	....	..	7 35	..	8 14	....	8 26	....	8 51	....	9 7	9 38	....	10 15
Great Missenden	..	..	7 1	7 16	..	....	7 44	....	8 23	..	8 35	..	9 1	..	9 16	9 47	..	10 24
WENDOVER	§5 0	....	7 10	7 25	....	..	7 53	..	8 32	....	....	....	A9 13	....	9 25	9 56	....	10 33
STOKE MAND'VILLE	..	..	7 15	..	..	....	7 58	....	8 37	..	..	..	..	..	9 30	10 1	..	10 38
AYLESBURY	5 12	....	7 20	7 33	....	..	8 3	..	8 42	....	....	....	9 21	....	9 35	10 6	....	10 43

*–Change at Wembley Park. ‡–Through train from City. ¶–First and third class.
§ Sets down only. A–Arrives 4 minutes earlier.

LONDON - HARROW - AMERSHAM - AYLESBURY **Metropolitan Line Table 1**

All trains third class only except where otherwise stated.

SATURDAY–continued

No. 6.

Marylebone	..	10 0	....	‡	10 15	‡	....	....	‡	....	11 30	....	..	‡	‡	12 25	....	12 34
Baker Street	9 49	¶	..	10 5	..	10 36	10 47	11 6	11 15	11 21	..	11 47	..	11 58	12 12	..	..	..
Harrow-on-the-Hill	10 11	10 19	.:	10 23	10 34	10 57	11 6	11 27	11 34	11 42	11 48	12 9	....	....	12 34	....	....	12 52
Pinner	10 16	Restaurant Car	....	..	10 41	11 2	..	11 32	..	11 47	11 55	12 14	..	..	12 40	..	..	12 58
Northwood	10 22		..	....	10 50	11 8	....	11 38	....	11 53	12 4	12 20	....	....	12 46	12 55	....	1 3
Moor Pk. & Sandy Lodge	10 25		....	10 33	10 53	11 11	11 16	11 41	11 44	..	12 7	12 23	..	12 26	12 49	12 58	..	1 6
Rickmansworth	..		..	10 40	10 59	....	11 23	....	11 51	....	12 12	....	....	12 33	....	1 3	....	1 12
Chorley Wood	....		....	10 48	11 7	..	11 31	..	11 59	..	12 20	..	..	12 41	..	..	..	1 20
Chalfont & Latimer	..		..	10 55	11 15	....	11 38	....	12 6	....	12 27	....	....	12 48	....	....	....	1 28
Chesham arr.	....		....	11 6	11 30	..	..	..	12 17	..	..	..	..	12 59	..	..	..	1 37
Amersham	..		..	11 2	11 22	....	11 45	....	12 13	....	12 34	....	....	12 55	....	1 19	....	....
Great Missenden	....		....	11 11	11 31	..	11 54	..	12 22	..	B12 47	..	..	1 4	..	1 28	..	..
WENDOVER	..		..	11 20	11 40	....	12 3	....	12 31	....	12 55	....	....	1 13	....	1 37	....	....
STOKE MAND'VILLE	....		....	11 25	11 45	..	12 8	..	12 36	..	..	..	..	1 18	..	1 42	..	..
AYLESBURY	..	11 0	..	11 30	11 50	....	12 13	....	12 41	....	....	....	....	1 23	....	1 47	....	....

No. 7.

Marylebone	‡	‡	....	1 0	‡	‡	....	1 38	....	‡	....	....	‡	....	‡	....	3 20	‡	....	3 50	....
Baker Street	12 38	12 49	.	..	1 8	1 19	..	¶	1 39	1 50	..	2 1	2 13	2 35	2 45	3 6	¶	3 23	..	..	4 6
Harrow-on-the-Hill	12 59	....	....	1 18	1 29	....	....	1 57	2 2	2 9	....	2 23	2 32	2 57	3 4	3 27	3 39	3 41	....	4 8	4 29
Pinner	1 5	..	..	1 25	1 35	..	..	2 4	2 8	..	..	2 29	..	3 2	..	3 32	Restaurant Car	..	..	4 14	4 34
Northwood	1 11	....	....	1 34	1 42	....	....	2 11	2 15	....	....	2 35	....	3 8	....	3 38		....	....	4 20	4 40
Moor Pk. & Sandy Lodge	1 14	1 17	..	1 37	1 45	1 48	..	2 14	2 18	2 21	..	2 38	2 42	3 11	3 14	3 41		3 51	..	4 23	4 43
Rickmansworth	....	1 24	....	1 43	....	1 55	....	2 20	....	2 29	....	....	2 50	....	3 22	....		3 59	....	4 28	....
Chorley Wood	..	1 32	..	1 51	..	2 3	..	2 28	..	2 37	..	..	2 58	..	3 30	..		4 7	..	4 36	..
Chalfont & Latimer	....	1 39	....	1 59	....	2 10	....	2 35	....	2 45	....	....	3 5	....	3 37	....		4 14	....	4 43	....
Chesham arr.	..	1 50	..	..	..	2 21	..	..	..	2 54	..	..	3 16	..	3 49	..		4 25	..	4 54	..
Amersham	....	1 46	....	2 6	....	2 17	....	2 43	....	....	....	....	3 12	....	3 44	....		4 21	....	4 50	....
Great Missenden	..	1 55	..	2 15	..	2 26	..	2 52	..	..	..	..	3 21	..	3 53	..		4 30	..	4 59	..
WENDOVER	....	2 4	....	2 24	....	2 35	....	3 1	....	....	....	....	3 30	....	4 1	....		4 39	....	5 8	....
STOKE MAND'VILLE	..	2 9	..	2 29	..	2 40	..	3 7	..	..	..	..	3 35	..	4 6	..	..	4 44	..	5 13	..
AYLESBURY	....	2 14	....	2 34	....	2 45	....	3 12	....	....	....	....	3 40	....	4 11	....	4 20	4 49	....	5 18	

‡–Through train from City. ¶–First and third class. B–Arrives 5 minutes earlier

One of the former Great Central 4-6-0's in LNER days near Dutchlands summit with a through train to the Midlands. During the 1920's and 1930's the area north of Rickmansworth was much more open, as here.

H C Casserley

LONDON - HARROW - AMERSHAM - AYLESBURY — Metropolitan Line Table 1

SATURDAY–continued — All trains third class only except where otherwise stated

No. 8.																				
Marylebone	....	4 50	5 0	....	....	....	....	....	6 8	....	....	....	....	....	....	....	....	....	9 32	....
Baker Street	4 23	¶	¶	4 53	5 8	5 21	5 38	5 51	¶	6 21	6 38	7 6	7 23	7 51	8 8	..	8 51	9 8	..	9 50
Harrow-on-the-Hill	4 42	....	....	5 17	5 27	5 44	5 57	6 14	....	6 44	6 57	7 29	7 42	8 14	8 27	....	9 13	9 27	9 50	10 14
Pinner	..		..	5 22	..	5 49	..	6 19	6 30	6 49	..	7 34	..	8 19	..	..	9 18	..	9 57	10 19
Northwood	....		....	5 28	....	5 55	....	6 25	6 36	6 55	....	7 40	....	8 25	....	....	9 24	....	10 6	10 25
Moor Pk.&Sandy Lodge	4 52		..	5 31	5 37	5 58	6 7	6 28	6 39	6 58	7 7	7 43	7 52	8 28	8 37	..	9 27	9 37	10 9	10 28
Rickmansworth	5 0		....	....	5 45	....	6 15	....	6 44	....	7 15	....	8 0	....	8 45	....	9 31	9 45	10 14	10 32
Chorley Wood	5 8	Restaurant Car	..	..	5 53	..	6 23	..	6 52	..	7 23	..	8 8	..	8 53	..	..	9 53	10 22	..
Chalfont & Latimer	5 15		....	....	6 0	....	6 30	....	6 59	....	7 30	....	8 15	....	9 0	9 27	....	10 0	10 29	....
Chesham ...... arr.	5 26		..	..	6 11	..	6 41	..	7 10	..	7 41	..	8 26	..	9 11	9 35	..	10 16	10 40	..
Amersham	5 22		5 45	....	6 7	....	6 37	....	7 6	....	7 37	....	8 22	....	9 7	....	....	10 7	10 36	....
Great Missenden	B5 42		5 54	..	6 16	..	6 46	..	7 15	..	7 46	..	8 31	..	9 16	..	..	10 16	10 45	..
WENDOVER	5 51		6 3	....	6 25	....	6 55	....	7 24	....	7 55	....	8 40	....	9 25	....	....	10 25	10 54	....
STOKE MAND'VILLE	5 56	..	6 8	..	6 30	..	7 0	..	7 29	..	8 0	..	8 45	..	9 30	..	..	10 30	10 59	..
AYLESBURY	6 1	5 48	6 13	....	6 35	....	7 5	....	7 34	....	8 5	....	8 50	....	9 35	....	....	10 35	11 4	....

No. 9.	SATURDAY–continued							SUNDAY										
Marylebone	....	10 45	....	....	....	....	12 45	....	....	....	8 15	..	....	9 50	....	....	....
Baker Street	10 0	¶	10 51	11 0	11 52	12 0	¶	*7 10	..	..	¶	9 2	9 15	¶	10 0	10 19	10 30
Harrow-on-the-Hill	10 22	....	11 14	11 22	12 14	12 22	....	7 40	....	....	8 34	9 25	9 35	10 9	10 20	10 40	10 49
Pinner	..	..	11 19	..	12 19	..	..	7 46	..	..	8 43	9 30	..		10 26	10 45	..
Northwood	....	....	11 25	....	12 25	....	....	7 52	....	....	8 53	9 36	....		10 33	10 51	....
Moor Pk.&Sandy Lodge	10 32	..	11 28	11 32	12 28	12 32	..	7 55	..	..	8 56	9 39	9 45		10 36	10 54	10 59
Rickmansworth	10 40	....	....	11 40	....	12 40	....	8 2	....	....	9 1	..	9 53		10 43	....	11 7
Chorley Wood	10 48	..	..	11 48	..	12 48	..	8 9	..	..	9 9	....	10 0		10 50	..	11 14
Chalfont & Latimer	10 55	....	....	11 55	....	12 55	....	8 16	8 40	....	9 16	..	10 7	Restaurant Car	10 57	....	11 21
Chesham ...... arr.	11 6	..	..	12 6	..	1 6	..	8 24	8 48	..	9 32	....	10 18		11 8	..	.
Amersham	11 2	....	....	12 2	....	1 2	....	....	....	....	9 24	..	10 14		11 4	....	11 28
Great Missenden	11 11	..	..	12 11	..	1 11	..	..	..	..	9 33	....	10 23		11 13	..	11 37
WENDOVER	11 20	....	....	12 20	....	1 20	....	....	....	....	9 42	..	10 32		11 22	....	11 46
STOKE MAND'VILLE	11 25	..	..	12 25	..	1 25	..	..	..	..	9 47	....	10 37	..	11 27	..	11 51
AYLESBURY	11 30	11 40	....	12 30	....	1 30	1 39	....	....	....	9 52	..	10 42	10 53	11 32	....	11 56

¶–First and third class. *–Change at Wembley Park. B–Arrives at 5 30 p.m.

LONDON - HARROW - AMERSHAM - AYLESBURY — Metropolitan Line Table 1

All trains third class only except where otherwise stated.

SUNDAY–continued

No. 10.																			
Marylebone	....	..	....	....	....	....	....	....	....	3 30	....	....	....	....	....	....	....	....	6 7
Baker Street	10 45	11 30	12 15	1 0	..	1 45	2 30	..	3 0	¶	3 45	..	4 30	..	5 15	..	5 49	6 0	¶
Harrow-on-the-Hill	11 5	11 50	12 35	1 20	....	2 5	2 50	....	3 21	3 50	4 5	....	4 51	....	5 36	....	6 10	6 20	6 28
Pinner	11 11	11 56	12 41	1 26	..	2 11	2 56	..	3 26	..	4 11	..	4 57	..	5 42	..	6 15	..	6 36
Northwood	11 18	12 3	12 48	1 33	....	2 18	3 3	....	3 33		4 18	....	5 4	....	5 49	....	6 21	....	6 47
Moor Pk. & Sandy Lodge	11 21	12 6	12 51	1 36	..	2 21	3 6	..	3 36		4 21	..	5 7	..	5 52	..	6 24	6 30	6 50
Rickmansworth	11 29	12 14	12 59	1 44	....	2 29	3 14	....	3 44		4 29	....	5 15	....	6 0	....	....	6 38	6 58
Chorley Wood	11 36	12 21	1 6	1 51	..	2 36	3 21	..	3 51	Restaurant Car	4 36	..	5 22	..	6 7	..	..	6 45	7 5
Chalfont & Latimer	11 43	12 28	1 13	1 58	....	2 43	3 28	....	3 58		4 43	....	5 29	6 3	6 14	....	....	6 52	7 13
Chesham ...... arr.	11 54	12 39	1 24	2 9	..	2 54	3 39	..	..		5 4	..	5 40	6 11	6 34	..	..	..	7 22
Amersham	11 50	12 35	1 20	2 5	....	2 50	3 35	....	A4 20		4 50	....	5 36	....	6 21	....	....	6 59	7 22
Great Missenden	11 59	12 44	1 29	2 14	..	2 59	3 44	..	4 29		4 59	..	5 45	..	6 30	..	..	7 8	7 31
WENDOVER	12 8	12 53	1 38	2 23	....	3 8	3 53	....	4 38		5 8	....	5 54	....	6 39	....	....	7 17	7 40
STOKE MAND'VILLE	12 13	12 58	1 43	2 28	..	3 13	3 58	..	4 43	..	5 13	..	5 59	..	6 44	..	..	7 22	7 45
AYLESBURY	12 18	1 3	1 48	2 33	....	3 18	4 3	....	4 48	4 33	5 18	....	6 4	....	6 49	....	....	7 27	7 50

No. 11																			
Marylebone	....	....	....	....	....	....	....	....	....	....	....	....	....	....	....	10 55	..	....	....
Baker Street	6 34	6 45	7 19	7 30	8 4	..	8 15	8 49	..	9 0	9 34	9 45	10 4	10 15	..	¶	10 49	11 0	..
Harrow on the Hill	6 55	7 5	7 40	7 50	8 25	....	8 35	9 10	....	9 20	9 55	10 5	10 25	10 35	....	....	11 13	11 22	....
Pinner	7 0	..	7 45	..	8 30	..	..	9 15	..	..	10 0	..	10 30	..	..	..	11 17	..	..
Northwood	7 6	....	7 51	....	8 36	....	....	9 21	....	....	10 6	....	10 36	....	....	....	11 23	....	....
Moor Pk.& Sandy Lodge	7 9	7 15	7 54	8 0	8 39	..	8 45	9 24	..	9 30	10 9	10 15	10 39	10 45	..	..	11 26	11 32	..
Rickmansworth	....	7 23	....	8 8	....	....	8 53	....	....	9 38	....	10 23	....	10 53	....	....	..	11 40	....
Chorley Wood	..	7 30	..	8 15	..	..	9 0	..	..	9 45	..	10 30	..	11 0	..	..	....	11 47	..
Chalfont & Latimer	....	7 37	....	8 22	....	....	9 7	....	....	9 52	....	10 37	....	11 7	....	....	..	11 54	....
Chesham ...... arr.	..	7 52	..	8 33	..	..	9 18	..	..	10 7	..	10 52	..	11 18	..	..	....	12 5	..
Amersham	....	7 44	....	8 29	....	....	9 14	....	....	9 59	....	10 44	....	11 14	....	11 37	..	12 1	....
Great Missenden	..	7 53	..	8 38	..	..	9 23	..	..	10 8	..	10 53	..	11 23	..	11 46	....	12 10	..
WENDOVER	....	8 2	....	8 47	....	....	9 32	....	....	10 17	....	11 2	....	11 32	....	11 55	..	12 19	....
STOKE MAND'VILLE	..	8 7	..	8 52	..	..	9 37	..	..	10 22	..	11 7	..	11 37	..	..	....	12 24	..
AYLESBURY	....	8 12	....	8 57	....	....	9 42	....	....	10 27	....	11 12	....	11 42	....	12 3	..	12 29	....

¶–First and third class. A–Arrives 4 4 p.m.

Crane truck at Neasden in 1930's.

H C Casserley

AYLESBURY - BRACKLEY - LEICESTER — **British Railways Table 2**

WEEKDAYS

						RC			③	RC	③ SO	SO	SX		RC	③ SX	③ SO	RC		③ SX
AYLESBURY *Joint*	5 15	....	....	....	9 25	11 2	....	....	11 54	....	1 52	3 17	3 30	....	4 22	5 25	5 23	5 49	6 18	6 55
QUAINTON ROAD	..	..	..	..	9 40	..	..	..	12 4	..	2 2	3 27	3 40	..	..	5 35	5 33	..	6 28	7 5
Calvert	....	....	....	....	9 50	....	....	....	12 13	....	2 11	3 37	3 50	....	....	5 43	....	....	6 38	....
Finmere	5 44	..	..	..	10 2	..	..	..	12 22	..	2 21	3 47	4 0	..	..	..	..	..	6 48	..
Brackley *Central*	5 53	....	....	....	10 11	....	....	....	12 31	1 37	2 30	3 55	4 8	....	4 48	....	....	....	6 57	....
Helmdon *ER*	..	..	..	..	10 21	..	..	..	..	....	..	4 5	4 18	..	..	..	..	..	7 8	..
Culworth	....	....	....	....	10 30	....	....	....	....	..	....	4 14	4 27	....	....	....	....	....	7 16	....
Woodford Halse	6 10	6 35	8 15	..	10 36	11 38	..	12 30	..	1 51	..	4 20	4 33	4 45	5 4	..	..	..	7 22	..
Banbury *Bridge St.*	....	....	8 42	....	....	....	....	12 48	....	..	....	....	....	5 15	....	....	....	....	....	....
Rugby *Central*	..	7 0	..	..	11 8	12 0	..	..	..	2 13	..	..	..	..	5 26	..	..	..	..	..
Leicester *Central*	....	7 47	....	....	11 47	12 25	....	....	....	2 38	....	....	....	....	5 51	....	....	7 0	....	....

WEEKDAYS—continued / SUNDAY

	SX	SO			SX		③ SO	SO						RC		RC			
AYLESBURY *Joint*	7 34	7 38	....	....	11 3	....	11 9	11 48	....	....	1 41	....	9 56	10 56	....	4 36	7 55	12 7	....
QUAINTON ROAD	7 44	7 48	..	..	..	..	11 20	..	..	..	..	..	10 6	..	..	..	8 5	..	..
Calvert	7 54	7 58	....	....	....	....	11 30	....	....	....	....	....	10 15	....	....	....	8 15	....	....
Finmere	8 4	8 8	..	..	..	..	11 40	..	..	..	..	..	10 24	..	..	..	8 25	12 32	..
Brackley *Central*	8 13	8 17	....	....	....	....	11 49	....	....	....	....	....	10 34	....	....	5 4	8 34	12 40	....
Helmdon *ER*	..	..	..	..	..	..	..	..	..	..	..	..	10 42	..	..	..	8 44	..	..
Culworth	....	....	....	....	....	....	....	....	....	....	....	....	10 51	....	....	....	8 54	....	....
Woodford Halse	8 31	8 35	9 29	..	11 43	12 3	..	12 28	..	12 43	2 26	3 20	10 57	11 35	12 18	5 21	9 0	12 59	..
Banbury *Bridge St.*	....	....	....	....	....	12 21	....	....	....	....	....	3 38	....	....	12 54	....	....	....	....
Rugby *Central*	..	..	9 49	..	12 6	.	..	..	..	1 3	2 45	..	11 22	11 57	..	5 43	..	1 23	..
Leicester *Central*	....	....	10 23	....	12 37	....	....	1 12	....	1 34	3 27	....	11 54	12 26	....	6 18	....	1 53	....

③—Third class only. RC—Restaurant Car. SO—Saturday only. SX—Saturday excepted.

British Railways local timetable for the service between Aylesbury and Leicester. It is remarkable now to think that places like Woodford, Culworth, Helmdon and Brackley had two route alternatives to London. Now they have only meagre road transport, as an alternative to the car.

LEICESTER - BRACKLEY - AYLESBURY — **British Railways Table 2**

WEEKDAYS

	MX	MX	MO	MX					RC		③		RC SO	RC		③ SO		③ SX	③ SO	③ SX
Leicester *Central*	2 15	2 39	....	....	6 20	....	7 20	....	11 30	....	....	....	1 11	2 21	....	....	2 26	....	....	....
Rugby *Central*	2 53	..	..	..	7 5	..	8 1	..	11 58	..	..	..	1 39	..	..	..	3 8	..	..	..
Banbury *Bridge St*	....	....	....	....	....	....	....	10 4	....	....	....	1 16	....	....	....	....	....	....	....	....
Woodford Halse	3 14	3 32	6 20	6 20	7 25	7 38	8 37	10 28	12 22	..	..	1 44	..	..	..	..	3 41	..	..	..
Culworth	....	....	6 27	....	....	7 45	8 44	....	....	....	....	....	....	....	....	....	3 48	....	....	....
Helmdon *ER*	..	..	..	..	..	7 53	8 52	..	..	..	..	..	..	..	..	..	3 56	..	..	..
Brackley *Central*	....	....	6 45	6 45	....	8 1	9 0	....	12 38	....	1 0	....	....	....	....	3 20	4 4	....	....	....
Finmere	..	..	6 54	6 54	..	8 10	9 10	..	..	..	1 9	..	..	..	..	3 29	4 14	..	..	..
Calvert	....	....	7 4	7 4	....	8 20	9 21	....	....	....	1 19	....	....	....	....	3 39	4 25	5 55	....	....
QUAINTON ROAD	..	..	7 12	7 12	..	8 28	9 29	..	..	..	1 27	..	..	..	..	3 48	4 33	6 3	6 30	7 20
AYLESBURY *Joint*	....	4 13	7 21	7 21	....	8 37	9 39	....	1 3	....	1 37	....	2 31	3 33	....	3 58	4 43	6 13	6 40	7 30

WEEKDAYS—continued / SUNDAY

		RC			SX				RC	③				RC					
Leicester *Central*	....	7 2	....	....	....	....	....	....	1 34	....	....	5 45	6 45	6 58	....	....	....	....	....
Rugby *Central*	..	7 30	..	..	..	..	..	..	2 4	..	..	6 22	..	7 33	..	..	..	..	..
Banbury *Bridge St.*	5 50	....	....	....	11 50	....	....	....	....	....	5 30	....	....	....	....	....	....	....	....
Woodford Halse	6 15	7 52	..	..	12 8	..	..	9 0	2 27	3 5	5 48	6 46	..	7 56	..	..	..	..	..
Culworth	....	....	....	....	....	....	....	9 7	....	3 12	....	....	....	....	....	....	....	....	....
Helmdon *ER*	..	..	..	..	..	..	..	9 14	..	3 19	..	..	..	..	..	..	..	..	..
Brackley *Central*	....	8 8	..	....	....	....	....	9 22	....	3 27	....	7 5	7 39	8 12	....	....	....	....	....
Finmere	..	..	..	..	..	..	..	9 32	..	3 37	..	..	..	..	..	..	..	..	..
Calvert	....	....	....	....	....	....	....	9 42	....	3 47	....	....	....	....	....	....	....	....	....
QUAINTON ROAD	..	..	..	..	..	..	..	9 51	..	3 56	..	..	..	..	..	..	..	..	..
AYLESBURY *Joint*	....	8 33	....	....	....	....	....	10 1	3 21	4 6	....	....	8 11	8 42	....	....	....	....	....

③—Third class only. MO—Monday only. MX—Monday excepted. RC—Restaurant Car. SO—Saturday only. SX—Saturday excepted.

73

Near Dutchlands summit B17 2867 'Bradford', one of the football club named engines, the half ball is visible on the nameplate.
Jack Turner

Index

Postscript to Volume 1

Five miles north of Baker Street in August 1880 at Kingsbury & Neasden. A remarkable photograph showing the station within a week of opening. One of 'A' class cabless locomotives with a train of early Metropolitan stock for Harrow. It is a striking example of how rural the area was when the railway first arrived.

Railway Magazine

Bibliography for volumes 1 and 2

THE SECOND RAILWAY KING The Life and Times of Sir Edward Watkin 1919-1901 by David Hodgkins 2002, Merton Priory Press Ltd

LONDON'S METROPOLITAN RAILWAY by Alan A Jackson 1986, David & Charles Inc

STEAM TO SILVER by J Graeme Bruce, London Transport Executive

MET & GC JOINT LINE an OBSERVER'S NOTES by Albin J Reed

RAF HALTON RAILWAY by Tony Coldwell

LONDON AND ITS RAILWAYS by R Davies and M D Grant, David & Charles Inc

THE ROMANCE OF LONDON'S UNDERGROUND by W J Passingham, Sampson Low, Marston & Co Ltd

THE RAILWAYS OF UXBRIDGE by C T Goode

WALTER ATKINSON-BUILDER OF THE HARROW AND UXBRIDGE RAILWAY by Dennis Edwards in UNDERGROUND magazine of the London Underground Railway Society

THE HARROW & STANMORE RAILWAY by Peter G Scott

RAILWAY MAGAZINE various editions

Various publications and the work of the Buckinghamshire Railway Centre, Quainton Road station, Buckinghamshire

Details of Locomotives and tables for Metropolitan included in volume 1 of this history

Apologia

The author would like to apologise for errors made in the first volume of this history which are as follows:.

Page 5 Acknowledgments, read Colour-Rail for Colorviews

Page 10 col 1 sixth line from bottom, The temporary terminus of the Great Northern Railway was Maiden Lane not Maiden Vale.

Page 47, 48, 49 col Sir Edward Watkin was Chairman of the South Eastern Railway not the South Eastern & Chatham. The South Eastern Railway did not become part of the South Eastern & Chatham until August 1898, by which time Watkin had left the board.

Page 135 Class G locomotive see 0-6-4T for 0-6-2T

Lamplight Railway Publications

Journeys in Time

A History of the Metropolitan Railway Volume 1
The story of the famous London Circle line and the branch to Hammersmith. Also the extension north from Baker Street to Rickmansworth. The text is supported with over two hundred half tone, some colour and diagrammatic illustrations. Contains classification of motive power for this railway. Two volumes to follow will carry the line to Aylesbury and Verney Junction. 160 pages, full colour reinforced laminate cover
£17.95 plus p&p £2.50

The Oxford to Cambridge Railway
Forty Years On 1960 - 2000
Following on from Bill Simpson's Oxford Cambridge Railway histories in the eighties to look how the line has changed. 144 pages, full colour laminate cover. **£12.95 plus p&p £2.00**

A History of the Stratford-upon-Avon and Midland Junction Railway
This superb volume of a cross country route from Broom Junction to Olney is contained in 160 pages. Over two hundred photographs, line illustrations, maps, etc. A must for anyone interested in the railways in Northamptonshire, Warwickshire and Oxfordshire. **£24.95 plus p&p £2.50**

A History of the Railways of Oxfordshire
Part 1: The North
First of a two volume history of Oxfordshire railways complete with over 250 photographs, maps, diagrams and text. Also unique personal accounts from former railway employees. Included are the ironstone works railways and the Bicester Military Railway related in 192 pages.
£19.95 plus p&p £2.50

A History of the Railways of Oxfordshire
Part 2: The South
South of Oxford lines, with over two hundred photographs, maps and disgrams. Oxford, Thame and Princes Risborough; the Watlington and Abingdon Branches and the Wantage Tramway in 192 pages
£19.95 plus p&p £2.50

The Wolverton to Newport Pagnell Branch
A fascinating branch line history with over a hundred photographs, maps, diagrams, timetables and an additional section on the Wolverton & Stony Stratford Tramway. **£8.95 plus p&p £1.25**

The Dunstable Branch
Branch line of the LNWR that was later extended to Luton by the Great Northern Railway. over a hundred photographs, maps, timetables, diagrams in 143 pages. Also covering the narrow gauge sand quarry railway, now the preserved Leighton Buzzard Narrow Gauge Railway **£8.95 plus p&p £1.25**

The Banbury to Verney Junction Branch
Twenty-one mile branch from Verney Junction to Banbury, stations of Buckingham and Brackley in a hundred photographs, with maps, timetables and plans in 176 pages. A very interesting book of the people working on the branch. Some as far back as early 1900's. **£8.95 plus p&p £1.25**

All available from:

Lamplight Publications

260 Colwell Drive, Witney, Oxfordshire, OX28 5LW
Tel 01993 201182 Fax 01993 201182